GROUP PSYCHOTHERAPY WITH ADULT CHILDREN OF ALCOHOLICS
Treatment Techniques and Countertransference Considerations

MARSHA VANNICELLI

Director, Appleton Outpatient Clinic, McLean Hospital
and
Associate Professor, Harvard Medical School

THE GUILFORD PRESS
New York   London

© 1989 The Guilford Press
A Division of Guilford Publications, Inc.
72 Spring Street, New York, NY 10012

Printed in the United States of America

Last digit is print number: 9 8 7 6 5 4 3 2 1

Library of Congress Cataloging-in-Publication Data

Vannicelli, Marsha.
    Group psychotherapy with adult children of alcholics.

    bibliography: p.
    Includes index.
    1. Adult children of alcoholics.   2. Group psycho-
analysis.   3. Countertransference (Psychology)   I. Title.
[DNLM: 1. Alcoholism.   2. Countertransference
(Psychology).   3. Family.   4. Psychotherapy.   Group—
methods.   WM 430 V268g]
RC569.5.C63V36   1989   616.86'1   89-7551
ISBN 0-89862-167-4

Portions of this book were developed from a chapter entitled, "Group
Psychotherapy with Adult Children of Alcoholics," in *Group Psychotherapy: A Practitioner's Guide to Interventions with Special Populations,* edited by M. Seligman and L. A. Marshall. © 1989 by The
Psychological Corporation. Used by permission.

Acknowledgments

Many people have played an important role in this project — by adding to my knowledge, by providing support and encouragement, and by collaborating with me on the clinical content that has been developed in the manuscript.

Special thanks are owed to my editor, Howard Blane, Ph.D., who believed in me and the possibility of my successfully completing this project long before I believed his faith was warranted, and to my friends and colleagues who generously provided thoughtful clinical commentary and editorial assistance: Dale Dillavou, Ph.D., Steve Tottingham, M.S.W., Roberta Caplan, Ph.D., Diana Dill, Ph.D., Terry Levin, M.S.W., Gerald Billow, J.D., Mellisa Shack, M.A., and David Schreier, B.A. — and, in particular, to Geraldine Alpert, Ph.D., who found no clinical or editorial issue too small to attend to, or too large to tackle with inventive and creative solutions. My typist Barbara Panza and my research assistants Elizabeth Perry and Denise Nelligan patiently attended to the many details of the manuscript without losing interest or enthusiasm. To them, I am also deeply grateful.

My gratitude is also extended to the many therapists, beginners as well as experienced clinicians, whom I have been privileged to supervise. Their candor in sharing moments of distress and pain (their own as well as their patients'), as well as their exhilarating moments of success, have made it possible for me to more fully understand the richness and complexity of the work that we do.

Finally, I wish to acknowledge the special contribution of the many patients, my own as well as those of my supervisees, who challenged us to view the world through their eyes and then, again, to broaden their perspective.

iii

The Guilford Substance Abuse Series

EDITORS

HOWARD T. BLANE, Ph.D.
Research Institute on Alcoholism, Buffalo

HERBERT D. KLEBER, M.D.
Connecticut Mental Health Center, New Haven

Contents

Foreword

In July, 1969, having just completed my psychiatry residency training, I came to Washington, D.C., to serve for two years in the Public Health Service. I was assigned to the Laboratory of Alcohol Research at the Center for the Prevention and Control of Alcoholism, which was administratively based in the National Institute of Mental Health. The Alcoholism Center consisted of a tiny administrative office located at NIMH headquarters and a medium-sized intramural research laboratory which focused primarily on investigating alcoholism as a vehicle for understanding basic biological processes. In 1969, that was the sum total of federal activity in alcoholism.

Within just one year, however, the political picture had changed dramatically. In 1970, Congress passed the "Comprehensive Alcohol Abuse and Alcoholism Prevention, Treatment, and Rehabilitation Act." A major component of that bill was the establishment of the National Institute on Alcohol Abuse and Alcoholism (NIAAA), which was given co-equal status in the federal mental health bureaucracy with NIMH. The establishment of the NIAAA represented a major turning point in governmental policy regarding alcoholism treatment. Alcoholism had now gone "public."

During the ensuing 20 years, alcohol use and abuse issues continued to command increasing public and professional attention. Public visibility was furthered by public service advertising campaigns focusing on responsible drinking themes, citizen groups devoted to the enactment of anti-drunk driving legislation, and growing concerns about adolescent alcoholism and drug abuse.

A striking consequence of greater public awareness and

changing perspectives regarding alcoholism was a dramatic increase in demand for alcoholism treatment services. Employees began instituting employee assistance programs in which employees were often faced with the choice of losing their jobs or going for treatment. Drivers convicted of a DWI offense, when given the choice between alcoholism treatment or a jail sentence, were similarly inclined to choose the former. Public advertising campaigns directed toward destigmatization of alcoholism also produced an increased demand for treatment and rehabilitation services.

It is against this background that a second major alcoholism "revolution" has now emerged—the phenomenon of Adult Children of Alcoholics (ACOAs). Almost entirely self-generated as a social phenomenon, shaped largely without guidance or input from mental health professionals, the ACOA movement has been one of the most astonishing social phenomena of the past several decades. Within a very short period of time, a vast network of self-help support groups, of local and national organizations, and of highly complex social and societal networks have built up around the concept of the "adult-child."

The appeal of the "adult-child" concept is at its core a simple one. People who for years had been blaming themselves for their psychological shortcomings and self-defeating tendencies, were now being encouraged to reframe their difficulties in an entirely different light. Their difficulties, they were now being told, were, to a significant degree, due to the consequences of having grown up in an alcoholic family.

That this message has been received with enthusiasm by so many offspring of alcoholic families is perhaps, in retrospect, not surprising. But it certainly caught the mental health field by surprise, since it was largely a lay movement, developing with only minimal input from mental health professionals and researchers. Thus, although we are now well along in the development of the ACOA movement, many mental health professionals remain confused as to the validity of the ACOA concept and are alternately defensive and baffled by the appeal and apparent "success" of this self-help movement. As a consequence, many professionals have decided to remain on the sidelines, leaving the direction of this movement to either its lay organizers or to a limited number of clinicians who have produced a series of quasi-authoritative books about the ACOA phenomenon and its treatment.

Many of these books are almost entirely anecdotal, suggesting that this field is either so new that no systematic data yet exist or that, if scholarly work is being done, it is largely irrelevant. For many mental health professionals, exposure to this growing literature has only increased the sense of disquietude and the tendency to feel as if one is a "stranger in a strange land." Yet such a conclusion would be an unfortunate one. It would clearly be a mistake for mental health professionals to conclude that they either did not have a meaningful place in the ACOA phenomenon or that they have to put aside their prior views and skills in order to work effectively with this clinical population.

What you are about to read is a book that will convince you that such a stance is neither necessary nor appropriate. Dr. Vannicelli's book, in my opinion, makes two essential points—first, that, despite the public perception that the "adult-child" phenomenon is an entirely new concept, specifically related to the problem of growing up in an alcoholic family, this perception is an erroneous one; and second, that it is entirely possible to take a tried and true treatment method [in this case Yalom's (1975) dynamic interactional group therapy model] and apply it successfully to the clinical needs of ACOAs.

Further, these two messages in combination also underscore why it is so critical that traditional mental health professionals become active players in the ACOA phenomenon. As Dr. Vannicelli points out, the ACOA construct is, in fact, well-grounded in psychodynamic theory. Consequently, this movement can easily be thought of as an extraordinary opportunity for mental health professionals to not only provide effective treatment services to a previously isolated clinical population, but also, through the provision of these services, to play a major role in attenuating cross-generational transmission of maladaptive and psychopathological behavior patterns. Because the ACOA concept is itself so firmly rooted in transactional dynamic theory, efforts to break into these intergenerational patterns of behavior are likely to bear fruit in diminished transmission not only of alcoholism but also of character pathology.

Thus, as Dr. Vannicelli walks us through the critical components of a psychodynamically oriented group psychotherapy approach for ACOAs, she helps us make the appropriate connections between the unique challenges of working with the ACOA population and the established guidelines for dynamic interactional group psychotherapy that have been gleaned from decades of clinical experience. This latter experience is a rich clinical tradition and its application to this particular clinical population should substantially enrich the experiences not only of the clients who avail themselves of such treatment, but also of the mental health professionals who become more engaged in the ACOA journey.

PETER STEINGLASS, M.D.

Preface

Therapists working with adult children of alcoholics in group psychotherapy range widely in terms of their professional backgrounds, extent of training, and credentials. Licensed professionals as well as many paraprofessionals have been drawn to this work. Level of experience of group leaders working with this population varies considerably as does their motivation for undertaking this work.

This book is aimed at four major populations of therapists:

1. Dynamically oriented professionals in the mental health field who have already had experience doing group psychotherapy with other populations and who wish to apply their group psychotherapy expertise to the ACOA population. These readers will already have a basic understanding of the ways in which the past influences current behavior and perceptions and will have some familiarity with the interactional group psychotherapy model of Yalom (1975).

2. Trained professionals who are currently treating ACOAs in individual psychotherapy and who are interested in exploring the possibility of expanding their practice to include dynamically oriented group psychotherapy, as well.

3. Therapists, both individual and group, at all levels of training who are interested in better understanding the ways in which countertransference issues influence their work with clients. These readers will have an opportunity to explore the countertransference impasses that have developed in their work and the ways in which understanding one's own countertransference reactions can be an asset in working with ACOA clients.

4. Paraprofessional counselors who will find many of the sections on therapist issues and countertransference relevant to their counseling work (even if they are not yet adequately trained to do psychodynamically oriented group psychotherapy), and who may be thinking about further training in the mental health field.

Many of the readers who journey with me through these pages will already have ACOA groups under way, and will no doubt be comparing their experiences to those that I share from my own clinical practice. Other readers will be less familiar with the ACOA population and will find in these pages answers to the many common questions that concern therapists beginning to work with this population. Such questions include:

1. What is the "core constellation" of the ACOA "syndrome" that the therapist needs to pay attention to; that is, what does the "typical ACOA" look like?
2. Do all, or most, ACOAs need treatment?
3. Are ACOAs sicker than other populations that are likely to enter an outpatient clinic?
4. Do ACOAs need a special kind of psychotherapy, or can more traditional forms of psychotherapy be adapted to this population?
5. Can ACOAs be treated in generic psychotherapy groups or do they need to be treated in specialty groups with other ACOAs?
6. What are the advantages and disadvantages of mixing ACOA patients in with non-ACOAs in therapy groups?
7. What does the concept of "recovery" mean with regard to ACOAs? How is this different or the same as our thinking about therapeutic growth with other populations; and how is it different from the notion of "recovery" in AA?
8. Is there a particular stance that the therapist should take with regard to the ACOA patient that differs from his style and position with non-ACOAs? That is, should the therapist do anything special or different when he realizes that he has an ACOA in treatment? Should

any particular stance be taken about the use of alcohol or drugs?

9. What should the therapist do if the ACOA has a drinking problem or is currently living with a substance-abusing significant other?
10. What are the advantages and disadvantages of the treatment of ACOAs by therapists who are themselves ACOAs?
11. What are the pros and cons of self-disclosure about the therapist's own ACOA history (or lack thereof)?
12. What basic information-base, training, and clinical expertise is necessary for the ACOA group therapist?

In attempting to answer these questions, I begin (Chapter 1) with an introduction to the ACOA literature, defining the population and pointing to myths and misconceptions, as well as frequently cited ACOA characteristics. Chapter 2 discusses the rationale for group psychotherapy with this population — describing some of the specific ways in which a dynamically oriented therapy group can be helpful for ACOAs. In Chapter 3, the reader is given an opportunity to consider some of the issues involved in deciding whether to do an ACOA group, and if so, how it will be set up and who will be in it. Chapter 4 deals with the actual beginning of the group, and Chapter 5 prepares the leader for themes that are likely to come up as the group continues. Chapters 6 and 7 focus on leader issues, beginning (Chapter 6) with an in-depth consideration of countertransference, and continuing (Chapter 7) with an exploration of additional leader issues that affect the work of the ACOA group therapist. In Chapter 8, leader techniques are suggested that may be useful in furthering the development of the group. Chapter 9 addresses the training and preparation of the ACOA group therapist from the standpoint of alcohol-related content areas that will be important for his effectiveness, as well as specific group psychotherapy training. Finally, Chapter 10 takes a brief look at research related to group psychotherapy with ACOAs and suggests areas for future investigation.

Because of the many rich opportunities to productively use therapist countertransference reactions to further the work of group therapy, as well as the potential hurdles if countertransference reactions are not attended to (particularly in this field where so many ACOA therapists are likely to be ACOAs themselves), I have given considerable attention to countertransference phenomena throughout this volume. Although a detailed definition of countertransference and exploration of its significance to the therapist's functioning is provided in Chapter 6, a brief definition here may be helpful.

Countertransference, by its most general definition, refers to all the feelings about the patient that the therapist experiences during and after seeing him (and perhaps even *before* the first meeting), and also may include feelings that the therapist has about *himself* that seem to occur in relationship to a particular patient or a particular therapy group. These kinds of feelings are a fact of life which are part of the experience of all therapists. If understood, they can be a tremendous asset in furthering the work of the therapy. If not understood, or recognized, these feelings often get in the way of successful therapeutic work.

Winnicott (1949) differentiates between two kinds of countertransference — objective and subjective. Objective countertransference refers to feelings that the patient induces in the therapist that are relevant to the patient's core conflicts. Understanding these feelings can be very useful to the therapist in clarifying aspects of the patient's inner life and ways of relating to others that might otherwise be hard to appreciate. Subjective countertransference, on the other hand, refers to feelings that the patient creates in the therapist that have to do with the therapist's own past and his own personal idiosyncracies. (We might also think of these reactions as a sort of "transference" that the therapist has to the patient.) These countertransference feelings, if not adequately attended to, get in the way of the therapeutic work.

Countertransference issues lie at the heart of most of our therapeutic slip-ups — blurring of boundaries, unempathic responses, difficulties hearing important themes, and problems in limit setting. Countertransference issues potentially affect nearly every aspect of group life, beginning with the therapists's feelings about setting up a group with a particular subset of his patients, and continuing with his handling of the pregroup interview, setting up and maintaining the therapeutic contract, and the therapist's ability to "hear" the clinical material and to respond appropriately. These issues will be addressed throughout Chapters 3 through 8, as we move from Chapter 3 (Deciding to Do A Group and Selecting Members), to Chapter 4 (Beginning the Group), to Chapter 5 (Group Themes), Chapter 7 (Leader Issues), and Chapter 8 (Leader Techniques). In addition, Chapter 6 addresses countertransference issues in a more detailed way, providing exercises to help the group leader assess the role of countertransference in his clinical work with various populations.

1
Introduction

In recent years, more and more adult children of alcoholics (ACOAs) are finding their way into treatment, having recognized as adults, that they are currently facing emotional and interpersonal difficulties which they attribute, at least in part, to the consequences of having grown up in an alcoholic family. That increasing numbers of ACOAs are finding their way to treatment settings is related to the convergence of a number of important developments. First, there has been a growing body of clinical literature, which, although largely impressionistic and anecdotal, addresses itself to the consequences in adulthood of having been raised by an alcoholic parent (Brown, 1988; Brown & Beletsis, 1986; Cermak & Brown, 1982; Gravitz & Bowden, 1984; Kern, 1985; Macdonald & Blume, 1986; Seixas & Levitan, 1984; Vannicelli, 1988; Wood, 1987). Second, empirical investigations of alcoholic families are beginning to document alcoholism's effects not only on the chemically addicted family member, but on the entire family system (Davis, Berenson, Steinglass, & Davis, 1974; Steinglass, 1979; Steinglass, Davis, & Berenson, 1977; Wolin, Steinglass, Sendroff, Davis, & Berenson, 1975). Finally, these clinical observations and research developments, though still in their preliminary stages, have been popularized by the proliferation of Al-Anon ACOA Groups and scores of self-help books available to the ACOA.*

The ACOA movement, by way of the "adult-child issues," forges a link between the substance abuse-recovery field (AA and

---

*References are provided in Chapter 9.

Al-Anon) and more traditional psychodynamically oriented thinking. Once alcoholic patients are relatively stabilized with respect to abstinence, often accomplished in groups that are labeled "recovery groups," as well as through AA and NA,* both therapists and patients often become interested in examining underlying character structure and long-standing issues. For the many alcoholics who grew up, themselves, in dysfunctional families this entails examination of the ways in which the patient's current behavior may relate to his past — in particular to issues from his family of origin. Along with this, patients and therapists also begin to expect more "psychotherapeutic work" and less work that is strictly supportive.

Not only has the ACOA movement bridged the gap between the alcoholism recovery field and psychodynamic psychotherapy; on a much larger scale, it has brought psychodynamic thinking (the idea that current problems, modes of interaction, and ways of adapting are related to early experiences in our families of origin) to a much broader lay audience. The "adult-child" syndrome, disseminated through the many lay texts available and 1988 media popularizations (Lead articles: *Newsweek, Time, L.A. Times, People Magazine*), has brought home an important message to millions of people, otherwise unfamiliar with the importance of these concepts. Clearly, psychotherapists, particularly psychodynamically oriented psychotherapists, have long been acquainted with the importance of the past as it gets repeatedly played out in our adult lives. But the ACOA movement has made these ideas readily available to scores of troubled people. Even many whose parents were not alcoholic readily identify because the ACOA concepts so clearly and simply state, and repeat, that the past (particularly our early experiences with our parents) continues to be replayed in the present. The simple, straightforward writing of the ACOA authors applies to a huge audience of would-be "adult-children," with parents of many kinds. As a therapist recently pointed out to me in reference to this issue, "As far as I'm concerned, ACOA stands for adult children of airheads." With this definition the ACOA books apply to all of us.

---

*Narcotics Anonymous.

Who Are the ACOAs?

Before embarking on a discussion of strategies and techniques for dealing with this population, it may be useful to more carefully examine who the people are that we are characterizing as ACOAs. There are estimated to be some 22,000,000 people in the United States who are the grown offspring (age 18 or older) of parents who have had alcohol problems (Russell, Henderson, & Blume, 1985). Many therapists treating this population share some basic beliefs about the characteristics of this population. These beliefs guide their work (and often are what interest them in this population in the first place). It would seem that an essential starting point would thus be to know more about who the people are that we are calling ACOAs.

In a later section, I will briefly review the literature in order to capture the flavor of current views regarding this population — but before I do, I would like to give you an opportunity to explore your own lists of "defining criteria" for ACOAs. Worksheet 1 includes many of the criteria listed by writers in the ACOA field to describe the "typical" ACOA. This worksheet also includes many of the criteria from the Bell Object Relations-Reality Testing Inventory (Bell, Billington, & Becker, 1985, 1986). The Bell inventory consists of 90 true/false items, 45 of which were adapted from patients' descriptions of their perceptions of relationships and their characteristic patterns of relating, and 45 of which reflect perceptions of reality and reality distortion. Subscales of this inventory have been shown to differentiate adults active in the community — voluntary board members of two organizations — from borderlines, and to differentiate among various subgroups of psychiatric patients.

Review each of the items on this check list and place a check in Column 1 for each item that you believe generally applies to the ACOAs that you work with. Then, in Column 3 do the same thing for the non-ACOAs. (For now, leave Columns 2 and 4 blank.)

WORKSHEET 1   Defining Characteristics of ACOAs and Non-ACOAs

Characteristics	ACOA Generally true (1)	(2)	Non-ACOA Generally true (3)	(4)
Difficulty with intimate relationships				
Difficulty finishing projects				
Constant need for approval				
Need to control others				
Feeling powerless in interpersonal situations				
Difficulty in making decisions				
Judging oneself unmercifully				
Difficulty having fun				
Feeling isolated, lonely				
Trying to ignore unpleasant events				
Taking self very seriously				
Dependent love involvements				
Difficulties with the opposite sex				
Feeling "different"				
Extreme loyalty				
Super responsible/irresponsible				
Impulsiveness				
Feeling unexplainably anxious				
Misreading the behavior of others				
Fear or avoidance of feelings				
Compulsive behavior				
Self-esteem based on views of others				
Denial of feelings				
Difficulty accepting reality				
Fear of losing control				
Lack of trust				
Giving into the needs of others				
Not knowing what normal is				
Fear of rejection				
Confusion about what is real				
Extreme sensitivity to others				
Overreaction to change				
Lying unnecessarily				

Having completed this, review the items listed in Worksheet 1 again, this time placing check marks in Column 2 to reflect at least a single instance in which an ACOA patient that you worked with demonstrated a trait that you did not mark in the "generally true for ACOAs" column. Do the same for non-ACOAs in Column 4.

Most readers will probably find that while their "generally true" list of ACOAs and non-ACOAs initially differed, when they stretched their sights a little, similarities emerged between the two lists. This is not surprising, since people who come with emotional pain, seeking psychotherapy, usually share a basic handful of maladies that characterize the human condition. The extent to which this is so may be reinforced not only by what you have observed from your own list, but by examining the original source of the items that were listed in Worksheet 1 (see Table 1 Source of Defining Characteristics).

TABLE 1 Source of Defining Characteristics: Bell Inventory or ACOA Authors

Characteristics	ACOA Authors	Bell Inventory
Difficulty with intimate relationships	X	X
Difficulty finishing projects	X	
Constant need for approval	X	X
Need to control others	X	X
Feeling powerless in interpersonal situations		X
Difficulty in making decisions	X	X
Judging oneself unmercifully	X	
Difficulty having fun	X	
Feeling isolated, lonely	X	X
Trying to ignore unpleasant events	X	X
Taking self very seriously	X	
Dependent love involvements	X	X
Difficulties with the opposite sex		X
Feeling "different"	X	
Extreme loyalty	X	X
Super-responsible/irresponsible	X	

(cont.)

TABLE 1 (cont.)

Characteristics	ACOA Authors	Bell Inventory
Impulsiveness	X	
Feeling unexplainably anxious	X	X
Misreading the behavior of others		X
Fear or avoidance of feelings	X	
Compulsive behavior	X	
Self-esteem based on views of others	X	
Denial of feelings	X	
Difficulty accepting reality	X	X
Fear of losing control	X	
Lack of trust	X	X
Giving in to the needs of others	X	X
Not knowing what normal is	X	
Fear of rejection	X	X
Confusion about what is real	X	X
Extreme sensitivity to criticism	X	X
Overreaction to change	X	
Lying unnecessarily	X	

What does this exercise show? Hopefully, it will underscore the ways in which you differentiate ACOAs from non-ACOAs in your own thinking — phenomena that probably also influence to a considerable extent your reactions to the ACOA population, as well as countertransference "slippage." (This "slippage" will be discussed in Chapter 6.)

These exercises should also help to underscore that generalizations about ACOAs need to be made with considerable care. What seems clear, however, is that ACOAs, to differing extents, have had to contend with a variety of problems that frequently occur in alcoholic families such as: inconsistent parenting, with unpredictable rules and limits; chaotic or tense family environments; poor communication, with unclear messages and broken promises; and loneliness and isolation, as family members attempt to hide the family's problems and reduce the potential for shame and embarrassment. In short, for many children who grow up with an alcoholic parent (as may also be true for children who live with other kinds of disabled or dysfunctional parents) the parent's illness often takes center stage and depletes the family's ability to adequately meet the physical and emotional needs of the developing child.

Children growing up with these kinds of stresses develop coping mechanisms which allow them to adapt to an unpredictable and often chaotic childhood. Although the potential array of adaptive strategies and defenses that the child may develop is quite extensive, with considerable variability from one child to the next (Brown, 1988; Burk & Sher, 1988; Hibbard, 1987; Wilson & Orford, 1978), many authors (Beletsis & Brown, 1981; Black, 1981; Cermak & Brown, 1982; Gravitz & Bowden, 1984; Seixas, 1982; Wegscheider-Cruse, 1985; Woititz, 1983, 1985) have attempted to identify "typical" patterns of dysfunction characteristic of the ACOA, along with personality traits that each believes typifies this population. Although these lists vary considerably and cover a total range of nearly 30 characteristics (see Worksheet 1), few of which have been empirically verified, the lists at least help to highlight the tremendous range of possible problems.

The most commonly cited problems include: (1) difficulty with intimate relationships (Ackerman, 1987; Black, 1981; Cermak & Brown, 1982; Gravitz & Bowden, 1984; Wegscheider-Cruse, 1985; Woititz, 1983); (2) lack of trust in others (Black, 1981; Cermak & Brown, 1982; Gravitz & Bowden, 1984; Greenleaf, 1981; Seixas, 1982; Wegscheider-Cruse, 1985); (3) fear of loss of control (Black, 1981; Cermak & Brown, 1982; Gravitz & Bowden, 1984); (4) conflicts over personal responsibility, characterized by super-responsible and/or super-irresponsible behavior (Ackerman, 1987; Black, 1981; Cermak & Brown, 1982; Gravitz & Bowden, 1984; Greenleaf, 1981; Wegscheider-Cruse, 1985; Woititz, 1983); (5) denial of feelings and of reality (Ackerman, 1987; Black, 1981; Cermak & Brown, 1982; Gravitz & Bowden, 1984; Greenleaf, 1981; Seixas, 1982; Wegscheider-Cruse, 1985); (6) proclivity toward uncompromising self-criticism (Ackerman, 1987; Black, 1981; Cermak, 1985; Woititz, 1983); and (7) problems with self-esteem (Black, 1981; Cermak, 1985; Gravitz &

Bowden, 1984; Greenleaf, 1981; Wegscheider-Cruse, 1985; Woititz, 1983).

A number of writers have also described particular constellations of family roles adopted by many children of alcoholics which, they propose, are used to defend against painful feelings and to create some semblance of stability in the family and within the child. Wegscheider-Cruse (1985), for example, suggests that the most commonly adopted roles include those of "hero," "scapegoat," "lost child," and "mascot." Similarly, Black (1981) proposes "the responsible one," "the acting-out child," and "the adjuster."

It is important to point out that such lists of roles and personality traits, while possibly useful in helping us to organize our thinking about ACOAs, can also lead to stereotyped thinking and a failure to attend to the diversity of circumstances and the variety of adaptations that are possible. As Beletsis and Brown (1981) appropriately point out, the dynamics of family life may vary considerably depending on such factors as: (1) whether one or both parents are alcoholic; (2) the child's age when parental alcohol use becomes problematic; (3) the family's economic stability; and (4) the availability and use of external support systems. In addition, we might add the differential effects on the ACOA's development of: (1) the duration and severity of the alcoholism; (2) the number of generations of alcoholism in the family; (3) whether the alcoholic parent, as well as other family members, receive treatment around the alcohol issues; (4) whether the alcoholic parent is successful in recovering from alcoholism; (5) whether other serious psychiatric illness or substance abuse exists in the family; (6) whether sexual or physical abuse is part of the picture; and (7) the resources and coping skills of the nonalcoholic parent. In summary, while caution must be exercised in talking about the "typical ACOA," parental substance abuse often creates serious family disruption, and the growing child must develop coping strategies to deal with it.

While we can, to some degree, characterize the stresses that are frequently present in this kind of dysfunctional family, it is harder, by far, to characterize the "typical" product of such a family. Substance-abusing parents differ enormously in terms of patterns of abuse, personality strengths, psychopathology, defensive styles, and coping patterns. Increasingly, researchers and clinicians in the field of alcoholism refer to "the alcoholisms" rather than simply to alcoholism (Zucker, 1987). This is intended to capture the tremendous variation in terms of the course of alcoholism and the diversity of the individuals that it affects. Similarly, it is important to recognize that children growing up in families in which there is substance abuse — even if they are reacting to many of the same kinds of family disruptions — will develop different defensive structures to deal with them, and that the degree to which children are able to shelter themselves from the negative impact of parental alcoholism may vary enormously. In fact, there is increasing evidence that many ACOAs may grow up to be well-adjusted (Barnard & Spoentgen, 1986a, 1986b; Jacob & Leonard, 1986), despite the difficulties they have encountered in childhood (or, perhaps, *because of* the coping skills that they have developed). Other ACOAs will be less fortunate, and the coping strategies developed to sustain survival during childhood may become dysfunctional once the child becomes an adult. These ACOAs may need help undoing some of the overlearned patterns of their past.

In short, there are probably many "alcoholisms" and many different ways of being an ACOA. Clearly, the character structure, defenses, and personality types among ACOAs would be expected to be at least as varied as these factors would be in the alcoholic parents themselves. To paint this picture a bit more vividly, one might ask whether an ACOA who had an alcoholic father who recovered when she was a baby would be likely to experience the same kind of emotional dysfunction, course of treatment, or clinical outcome as an ACOA whose mother and father both drank throughout her childhood, or whose parents both drank until dad died of alcoholism when the child was nine. Similarly, one might wonder whether an alcoholic father, who recovered when his child was two, would produce an offspring who was more "typically ACOA" and more likely to fit the "typical syndrome" than a child whose mother had manic-depressive illness throughout his childhood. Equally interesting to consider is the degree of similarity between, for example, President Ford's children, and the quality of their lives in response to their mother's alcoholism, and a child growing up with an alcoholic mother in a one-parent, poverty-stricken family. It is clear that there is tremendous variability *within* the ACOA population and probably considerable overlap between clinical ACOA populations and other clinical non-ACOA populations who have suffered through some of the same kinds of unpredictable and erratic parenting.

Although the "core constellation" of the adult-child "syndrome" remains empirically undocumented, what does seem to be shared, at least by those ACOAs who find their way into treatment, is an awareness that their family lives were dysfunctional in significant ways which now affect the ACOA's adult functioning. While such a view of oneself and one's family of origin is probably shared by members of many other clinical populations who have grown up in dysfunctional families, what may be special for the ACOA is that the current focus on this form of family dysfunction may provide, for the first time, a sense that his or her problems can be labeled and remediated.

The Self-Definition of the ACOA Upon Presentation to Treatment

The ACOA movement, and in particular the presence of ACOA groups, provides an opportunity for many adults from dysfunctional families to find a way into treatment. The sense that "something is wrong," that others may share similar problems, and that the problems of the past (in growing up in their own family of origin) are the cause of current problems in relating to others and in living full lives, are all brought into focus by the growing movement toward ACOA treatment. For many, the ACOA focus provides a comfortable entree into treatment that might otherwise not be available.

On the negative side, the presence of specialized ACOA programs and therapy groups may foster the myth that issues related to being an "adult-child" can be dealt with *only* in a specialized ACOA group. Although there are clearly advantages to having ACOAs together in a group, any dynamically oriented therapy group would include as part of its task the work of examining the ways in which the past (and clearly relationship to parents is an essential part of this) influences the present. It is important to recognize that an ACOA therapy group is a *therapy* group and that "adult-child" issues are an essential part of this as well as any other dynamically oriented therapy. This is perhaps highlighted by an amusing case which recently came to my attention.

> *A young woman arrived for treatment at a substance-abuse clinic, posing as her presenting problem the need to "work on her adult-child issues." When the clinician inquired which of her parents had had the alcohol problem, the patient responded, "Why, neither." "How is it then," the interviewer inquired, "that you have come to this clinic for help?" "Oh," responded the client, "I've read all the ACOA books, I really identify with the issues, and I feel that I'm now ready to address them."*

This patient implicitly understood that "adult-child" issues were an important part of understanding herself and the intrapsychic and interpersonal problems that she was experiencing. She was misguided only in assuming that she would need to go to a specialized ACOA group to address them.

A similar kind of identification with the ACOA movement was evident in another patient's recent comment, "I think of myself as an 'adult-child' of a dysfunctional family. I only wish my parents had been alcoholics so I'd have something clear to focus on."

2
Rationale for Group Psychotherapy with ACOAs

The Interactional Group Therapy Model

The group therapy model that forms the frame of reference for this book is the dynamic interactional therapy model, which has been described in detail by Yalom (1975). It is similar to the Stanford ACOA group therapy approach described by Cermak and Brown (1982) and Brown and Beletsis (1986), with the exception that leaders do not mail out written summaries to group members after each session.

The group format involves weekly 90-minute sessions with eight to ten members who come together to explore their interpersonal relationships within a group. Group members are encouraged to explore in depth their style of relating to the leader(s) and other members by interacting freely and honestly in the immediate present while at the same time assuming a self-reflective pose. The group is seen as a special social microcosm in which basic feelings and life themes replay themselves and can be worked through. The group's task is to help members better understand and alter self-defeating ways of relating so that more meaningful relationships can be established. We view this kind of group therapy as a particularly helpful modality for ACOAs, and often the treatment of choice for a number of reasons.*

---

*Many of these advantages of group psychotherapy have also been addressed with regard to the treatment of alcoholic couples in Vannicelli (1987).

Reducing the Sense of Isolation

The grouping together of people who have identified themselves as ACOAs provides an initial sense of shared experience, thus increasing the possibility for initial bonding. The group presents at least the possibility of belonging and of being understood. This is critically important to offset the feelings of isolation that are common in those who have grown up in dysfunctional families. Although this may be one of the helpful aspects of group work for any population, it is particularly important for ACOAs. The stigma of the familial alcohol problem, and consequent feelings that family secrets should not be disclosed, increases the likelihood that little sharing has been done with others about the troublesome aspects of their family lives. Thus, the ACOA is likely to feel especially alone and different. As an ACOA patient in her individual therapy said about her boyfriend, "I've never had a normal relationship before. I don't know what it is. I feel crazy at times and really scared of letting him get close." Referral to a group with other ACOAs helped this young woman realize that she was not crazy but, rather, experiencing some understandable human emotions.

Instilling Hope

The ACOA group provides an opportunity to see others who are getting better. Members often experience a sense of hope when others in the group talk, in the past tense, of problems that they are currently facing — communicating that these problems are something that they have known *in the past* but have now worked through. This is one advantage of a revolving-membership group in which the various members are at different stages in their treatment. However, even in a group where all members are in the early phases of treatment, the members will work through different problems at different rates and thus can provide areas of hope for one another.

Conversely, hope can also be instilled by the opportunity to judge one's own progress against the yardstick of others who are still stuck. It is not unusual to hear a patient reflect, upon listening to a newcomer in the group, "Hey, doesn't that sound familiar? Remember how I used to get stuck in that rut?"

Learning from Watching Others

The opportunity to watch other members in action who are struggling with similar kinds of conflicts is often useful in giving a clear view of the ways in which others get stalled at critical points. There is thus an opportunity to understand dysfunctional behavior and aborted communications by watching them being played out in the group.

Equally important, members model for one another *useful* ways of communicating and interacting. By observing others, members thus have an opportunity to learn not only what does *not* work but also to get a first-hand view of *successful* interactions. Finally, the group provides a safe arena in which members can learn more about their own feelings and those of others, and how they can be most effectively communicated.

Altering Distorted Self-Concepts

Because of the potential in the group for examining one's own behavior in relationship to others (and getting group feedback), members have an opportunity to discover ways in which their self-images have been distorted, and the myths about themselves that continue to be perpetuated from the past. In addition, as members have an opportunity to identify with others and to accept them in spite of their flaws and secrets, they may also learn to be more accepting of these characteristics in themselves. As such, the group experience provides a healthy climate for the special sense of comfort that comes from seeing oneself and others in perspective.

Reparative Family Experience

Group therapy also offers the possibility of a reparative family experience. Not only does one have the opportunity to see one's family and one's role in it in greater perspective, but, as is often needed, new and healthier ways of relating are also learned. Long-term interactional group therapy provides an immediate "family context" in which to explore the past as it is recreated in the present. Particularly since many patients may experience their entry into treatment as an abandonment of their family of origin, the group serves as a substitute family that can be supportive during a process that is often experienced as difficult and painful. For the ACOA, the process of recovery involves a revision of the past. As Beletsis and Brown (1981) succinctly state,

> The facts of a childhood spent in a family with an alcoholic parent do not change. The memories remain detailed and vivid. However, the meaning attributed by the child to these events, gives way to a cognitive restructuring. Based on the validation of experience in a reparative therapeutic setting, this restructuring alters the belief system which mandated certain defenses as necessary to survival and allows for the development of more appropriate and adaptive defenses. (p. 31)

Understanding the Effects of Parental Alcoholism

Group psychotherapy offers the opportunity for learning along a number of fronts, and also for acquiring information about oneself in relationship to others (both in the past as well as in the present). As Wood (1987) points out, specific information and education about the effects of parental alcoholism are also important to the therapeutic work. This is not to be confused with the focus or intent of an education group; but, rather, the questions that we ask and our clarifications and interpretations provide information which can further group members' understanding of themselves in relationship to their past. As Wood points out, information about the effects of parental alcoholism is "frequently offered in the context of an interpretation, at a moment when the patient is or has recently been in the throes of an emotional conflict, so that a particular bit of information will likely elucidate the original source of the conflict" (p. 121).

This is nicely illustrated in a case example of a patient who had powerful wishes to "share his grief and fear" which were offset by equally powerful wishes to flee and to protect himself. Wood handled this by pointing out to the patient

> . . . that his struggles with his family around emotional sharing made his present struggle with himself quite understandable. I observed that alcoholic families frequently convey a powerful message to children that their needs for intimacy, support, and comfort are pathological, and I reassured him that, in fact, these feelings were a very human, and very valuable, part of him. (p. 139)

Aspects of Special Appeal

Group therapy may also appeal to the ACOA for two additional reasons, which are somewhat distinct from the therapeutic value of group for this population. First, an ACOA group provides a forum in which the patient may feel invited to *externalize* the source of his discomfort and pain by focusing on his problematic parent(s). And for people who have too long blamed themselves, this shift in focus may provide a source of initial relief. Thus, the ACOA problem may initially feel like a "circumscribed problem" and therefore manageable. It also provides what appears to be a single clear enemy — parental substance abuse — and a specific thing to blame. For many ACOAs the idea that something outside of themselves is bad and needs to be attended to is an easier focus on which to begin therapy. However, the idea of a single easy focus, "my ACOA issue," is soon dispelled because, in fact, the ACOA concerns involve all major issues that the patient faces, both present and past.

Second, ACOAs may find group therapy appealing because of the illusion that they can "hide out" in a group. Although patients may, in fact, enjoy rest periods, during which they may feel "safe" because they are not actively grappling with their own problems, important growth may occur while processing the work of others. This paradoxical "rest" is especially likely when issues that are being actively defended against in the "resting" member are being actively processed by another, thus giving the resting (defended) member an opportunity to gain vicariously as the other works. It is often the case, in fact, that a patient who is defending against his own problems may eagerly engage in helping another sort out issues that are closely related — not recognizing until later the relevance to his own experience as well.

Relationship of Group Therapy to Al-Anon and Al-Anon ACOA Groups

Along with the increasing interest in psychotherapy groups for ACOAs, there has been increasing interest and availability of self-help groups. In recent years, employee assistance programs have identified issues related to having grown up in an alcoholic family as a significant factor in many of their clients' physical and mental health problems. In such settings, peer groups (structured as self-help groups) have been used to help adult children of alcoholics understand and learn to deal constructively with their problems (Russell et al., 1985).

By far the most popular self-help groups, however, are the ACOA special interest groups of Al-Anon. This is a resource which has grown rapidly in the past few years, from only 14 registered Al-Anon ACOA groups in 1982 (Cermak, 1984) to 900 by 1987 (Krovitz, 1987). The focus of these groups is on the AA/Al-Anon 12 steps and 12 traditions of recovery, as well as more specifically on the problems of alcoholism as it relates to adult children. The program offers structure and support within the framework of the principles on which Al-Anon was founded.*

Thousands of adult children of alcoholics have found these self-help groups to be an invaluable source of support. Membership in a ACOA self-help program often occurs alongside of membership in a ACOA psychotherapy group, and work in the two can be mutually complementary. While many ACOAs find that the support they receive in their self-help programs adequately addresses their needs and issues, a psychotherapy group, led by a trained professional, offers a somewhat different kind of help. A leaderless group in which all members are participating, with the goal of self-help, is limited in the extent to which it can examine shared fallacies, group myths, and various kinds of intermember and group transference phenomena. In particular, the kinds of group themes that are detailed in Chapter 5, and which are often so important in understanding how the past is being relived in the present, are difficult to work through (let alone objectively observe) in a leaderless self-help group.

Since many patients entering an ACOA psychotherapy group will have had prior experience in some kind of self-help group, it is often helpful to clearly differentiate these two kinds of experi-

---

*Information about self-help resources is available through the following organizations: National Association for Children of Alcoholics, 31706 Coast Highway, Suite 201, South Laguna, CA 92677; National Council on Alcoholism, 12 West 21st Street, New York, NY 10010; and Children of Alcoholics Foundation, Inc., 200 Park Avenue, 31st Floor, New York, NY 10010.

ences, particularly the ways in which the expectations and ground rules differ, before bringing the patient into the group. These distinctions will be detailed further in Chapter 3.

In this chapter I have discussed some of the ways in which group therapy can be helpful to ACOAs. An ACOA group provides an opportunity to reduce one's sense of isolation, to instill hope, to learn from watching others, and to alter distorted self-perceptions. It also provides a unique opportunity to create a "family context" in which the past can be explored as it is recreated in the present. Finally, I have discussed the relationship between group psychotherapy and an ACOA or Al-Anon self-help group.

Having reviewed some of the advantages of these groups for the members, the next chapter examines some of the issues that the potential leader must consider before deciding to begin an ACOA therapy group.

3
Deciding to Do a Group and Selecting and Preparing the Members

The Decision to Begin

Before beginning an ACOA therapy group, therapists should feel comfortable exploring their motives for embarking on this venture. There are many good reasons for doing an ACOA group. Particularly for ACOA therapists, the wish to rescue or to help may be very great. Obviously there is much that is positive about this (for example, the ACOA's entrance into the field of psychotherapy). For many therapists there may also be a wish to give back to others what they themselves have received through the course of their own growth. Other positive reasons include the wish to learn and financial rewards. Less positive reasons are those related to unexplored wishes to treat oneself by setting up a group for "other ACOAs" or a sense of obligation (e.g., "Several of my ACOA patients are putting pressure on me to start a group").

It is important that your decision take account of your own needs and interests. While your patients' readiness for and interest in joining an ACOA group is also important to pay attention to, there are other options when you feel that a group placement would be desirable. For example, your patients might be referred to somebody else's group (if this doesn't feel like an option, it may be that you are having trouble letting go of some of your patients). It may also be possible to let your patients find their own ACOA groups. There are many such groups available today, and it is not unusual for patients to self-refer to these groups. It is important that you be open to exploring with your patients the thoughts and fantasies that they have had about joining an ACOA group, and, in particular, the thoughts and fantasies they have had about joining *your* group. It may be that when patients are putting pressure on the therapist to start a special group for ACOAs, that this has to do with transference issues that are coming up and the patients' wish to have the therapist create a family (the idealized family long yearned for).

When considering whether to begin an ACOA group the therapist must also consider whether to do so within his private practice or in conjunction with a substance-abuse outpatient clinic. Although many of the considerations concerning selection of patients, choosing a co-therapist, group size, etc., will be similar regardless of whether it is a clinic group or a private-practice group, there are also some important differences. ACOA groups that are set up as part of a substance-abuse clinic provide greater options for organized ancillary services for clients (individual, couples, and family therapy, along with the group treatment). Clinic ACOA groups may also offer a greater opportunity for sharing with colleagues and for supervision (peer or otherwise). In addition, a clinic ACOA group generally provides backup coverage when the therapist is away, as well as easy access to emergency backup when patients are in need of medication or hospitalization. Overall, ACOA groups that are set up in clinics are probably somewhat less stressful for the therapist and provide a greater cushion of support. However, they are also generally less financially rewarding and create other complications for the potential group leader, including coordination with clinic schedules and somewhat less flexibility in terms of client selection.

Regardless of whether the group is initiated in one's private practice or in a clinic, issues regarding group size and composition, duration of the group and whether time-limited or open-ended, need to be addressed before member selection and pre-screening actually begins. (The decision about whether or not to have a co-therapist, and criteria for selecting a co-therapist are also important to consider and are discussed later, in Chapter 8.)

Group Composition

In putting together a new group (or in replacing departing members), it is important to keep in mind certain guidelines about group composition. In selecting members for groups, both in our clinic (the Appleton Outpatient Clinic) and in my private practice, I use the principle of "maximal tolerable heterogeneity." In my experience, the group functions best and has the most potential for a rich array of dynamics when there is diversity among members. For this reason, whenever possible, I lean toward a mixed-sex group that spans an age range of more than one generation (i.e., some members will be old enough to be other members' parents), in which there is also a mix in terms of socioeconomic backgrounds, defensive styles, and diagnoses. Often the greatest richness is created when a new member is brought in who complements the dynamics of another (possibly because of a generational issue) or who, despite socioeconomic differences, is working on an issue similar to the group's focus (e.g., around intimacy and partnering, or difficulties in separating).

While greater heterogeneity has a positive impact in terms of enhancing the richness of the group and making it possible to more easily integrate a greater variety of new members, there are also limitations on heterogeneity that must be observed. Thus, a single "outlier" should be brought into a group only after cautious reflection. For example, if a group consists of married and divorced members in their late 30s to late 40s, one should think seriously about placing a single 22-year-old in such a group. If the leaders wish to diversify the group, they might consider bringing in two young unattached members so that neither would initially experience the sense of being all alone. Similarly, if a group has been composed of all female members and the leader wishes to make it a mixed-sex group, at least two men should be brought in. If one of the co-leaders is a male, it may be possible for a brief period of time to elapse before the second male member is introduced (but only if the entering male member is apprised in advance of his temporary outlier position).

Another limitation on heterogeneity relates to level of functioning of group members. An unemployed, highly withdrawn patient recently discharged from the hospital would not be appropriately placed in a high-functioning group. Similarly, a high-powered executive, even if paired with another high-functioning member, would generally not be well-suited to a group where most members were poorly functioning and still struggling to stabilize their work and personal lives. In my experience, however, leaders tend to err far more on the side of creating too much homogeneity than on the side of too much variation. Often, they are too cautious and protective of their groups, thereby restricting the group's vitality and potential (as well as its ability to absorb future members).

Finally, when a group becomes relatively homogeneous around a particular limitation of the patients (e.g., a group in which all members are relatively low-functioning, recently discharged inpatients), it may be appropriate to consider certain modifications in the structure of the group to accommodate these limitations. For example, with a low-level group the length of each session might be reduced (e.g., from 90 minutes to 50 minutes per session).

The Use of Conjoint Individual Therapy

Another important consideration concerns the use of individual therapy along with membership in an ACOA group. Possible variations include the following: (1) all members will be seen in individual therapy by the group leader (or one of the two leaders if co-led) along with participation in the group; (2) all members will be in individual therapy, as well as the ACOA group, but will be seen by therapists other than the group leader(s); (3) individual therapy will be optional, except in those cases in which the group leaders feel that individual therapy is essential along with membership in the group. Each of these possibilities has a different set of implications for group members and should be carefully considered prior to forming the group.

If it is the group leader's wish that all members be seen in individual therapy along with the ACOA group, it is generally preferable that a decision be made in advance either that all patients will be seen by the leader (or co-leaders) of the therapy group or that none will be. When the leader sees some of the group members individually but not others, a situation is fostered in which some members truly have "special" status with regard to the leader(s). Concerns about who the leaders care most about, know the best, and are the most interested in are important issues in the life of the group. Providing a relatively uniform context in which either all patients are seen by the group leaders individually or none are, provides a cleaner screen on which to examine these issues.

A special issue that therapists should be attuned to if they decide to form a group in which all members will be seen by the group leader(s) individually concerns both the therapist's and patient's feelings about the therapist having "chosen" certain patients to join her new "special family" (i.e., the group). This issue has special meaning not only for the patient — the issues of being chosen or picked — but also for the therapist. Her new "family" and all the aspirations she has for it (giving them the reparative experience that she knows that they long for, and that she, in turn, wishes them to have) has powerful meaning for the therapist.

As one therapist put it, as she began to think about constituting her ACOA group, "I can't imagine putting any of my patients into my ACOA group unless they have first been with me at least a few years in individual treatment. I feel that they are entitled to at least some time with me alone before they have to share me." This therapist was working out her own feelings (and wishes) about creating a family situation in which the new baby would have mother all to itself for a few years before having to even *watch* mother interacting with the other children in the family. Obviously this "ideal" is not frequently approximated in real life (and is likely only for the first born). However, this therapist's own countertransference feelings about the "family" that she was creating clearly came into play as she thought about various ways of constituting her new group. In fact, for members in such a group, issues around seeing "mother" interact with the other "siblings" will probably recreate very closely the family dramas from their own childhoods. For most children, watching mom interact with the other siblings and having to "share her" was a reality of their early lives.

If the decision about individual therapy is made on a case by case basis (some will have it, others will not) extensive individual therapy with the leader(s) should generally be avoided. On the other hand, the need for individual therapy may come up around a particular crisis for a group member — for example, when the group is moving quickly and a member is in a crisis of sufficient magnitude that the once-weekly group therapy sessions cannot sufficiently process and contain it. For brief periods (for example, one or two sessions), it may be useful for the group leader(s) to meet individually with the patient, with the understanding that the group knows about it and relevant information will be brought back into the group. As suggested above, if more extensive support is needed it would generally be advisable for the patient to be referred to another individual therapist.

Although I prefer the "all or none" model with regard to group members being in individual therapy with the group leader(s), such "ideal practices" may not always be possible. If the leader does find that he needs to be involved individually in a more extensive way with a patient, and there seems to be no reasonable alternative, it is important that the group know about this and be encouraged to talk about their reactions to it. It is important that this occur not only when the therapist's "special relationship" with a group member begins, but whenever it may be relevant throughout the course of the group.

There will be times after a patient has joined the group that concomitant individual therapy may become essential. Such is occasionally the case for patients who need the ongoing support of individual therapy in order to deal with the intense feelings aroused in the group. A need for individual therapy may also arise when a patient finds herself repeating a problematic role that so well matches an important group need that the group finds it difficult to help the patient out of the dysfunctional role. For example:

> In one group, a member thought of herself as the "star" in her family of origin and needed also to see herself as the group's shining success story. She found it extremely difficult to allow herself to truly engage as someone who needed help even when, with the help of the group, she had glimpses of things that she might work on. Because the group also needed a member to reflect the "group's

*success," they colluded in preventing her from engaging in any
serious work. Although the group, with time, did come to understand their collusion in this patient's defensive "success role"
and eventually got down to work, the concomitant use of an individual therapist would have been very helpful.*

Open-Ended versus Time-Limited Groups

When beginning a new group it is also important to consider the
advantages and disadvantages of open-ended versus time-limited
groups. The open-ended group offers the advantages of long-term
psychotherapy — allowing patients to stay as long as they need to
work through their issues. It also, however, requires a long-term
commitment on the part of the therapist who begins such a group.
When first beginning to work with ACOAs in groups, leaders
might want to consider a time-limited group, perhaps six months
to a year, in which most members begin together (or in near
proximity) and end together on a specified date. If the group is
time-limited, the group leader(s) should plan in advance the time
frame during which new members will be added. Options include:
(1) all members must be present the first night in order to join; (2)
new members will be allowed to enter over the course of the first
month; (3) the possibility of taking in new members will continue
throughout the year. These options should be considered in advance, and group members should be told specifically what the
operating ground rules will be. For example, though all members
entering such a group will understand that they are expected to
join the group for the entire course of the time-limited period, they
should also be told what will happen if for some reason a member
does drop out — that is, whether or not he will be replaced.

Member Selection and Prescreening

Careful clinical assessment is an essential part of the work to be
done before placing patients in ACOA therapy groups. As previously mentioned, for many patients the discovery that they are
ACOAs provides an entree into treatment — a discovery that is

particularly helpful for the many who might not have entered treatment otherwise, but who do, indeed, need help. However, while the patient's "self diagnosis" should be taken seriously, it should not get in the way of a more complete mental health assessment. This is particularly important with regard to the ACOA's own potential involvement with substance abuse, since the offspring of alcoholics are at three to four times greater risk for developing alcoholism themselves than are the offspring of nonalcoholics (Bohman, Sigvardsson, & Cloninger, 1981; Goodwin, Shulsinger, Hermansen, Guze, & Winokur, 1973; Schuckit, Li, Cloninger, & Deitrich, 1985), and are also at greater risk for marrying substance abusing partners (Black, 1981; Corder, McRee, & Rohrer, 1984; Gravitz & Bowden, 1984; Woititz, 1983).

In our clinic, ACOAs begin treatment with two or three individual evaluation sessions, followed by placement in a short-term (five-session, once-weekly) ACOA therapy group. Upon completion of both the individual evaluation and the five-week group experience, patients are then referred to one of our long-term, dynamically oriented ACOA groups, along with other psychotherapy — individual, couples, or family — as indicated.

At the beginning of the first evaluation interview, we recognize the patient's awareness of and discomfort around the "adult-child" issues and confirm our interest in addressing these concerns. We also point out that from our work with ACOAs we have learned that there are two other areas that are important to pay attention to from the outset — namely, that ACOAs frequently repeat the patterns of their past by marrying or settling in with a substance-abusing person, or by having concerns about their own substance use. Sometimes the latter occurs because there are, indeed, problems involving usage. Sometimes there is merely a need and a wish to know more about how one's own substance use fits into the patterns and repetitions of the past.

If the evaluator has concerns about the patient's current substance use or if it is clear that the patient is currently living with an active user, the patient is introduced to the concept of "hierarchical treatment." This term is meant to express the idea that the problem of highest crisis potential is treated first, while at the same time paying careful attention to the ACOA issue. If we do find that there is a substance-abuse problem, we tell the patient that we would like to treat this directly. He would then be referred to our clinic's substance-abuse track.* We would also let him know that the ACOA problem would certainly not be ignored (since roughly 50% of the substance abusers in treatment in our program are also adult children of alcoholics). Similarly, if the person is currently living with a chemically addicted other, he would be referred to our family track — again with the knowledge that if this person enters our family program and joins one of our long-term, dynamically oriented family members' groups, ACOA issues will be attended to, since 60 to 70% of the other participants will also be ACOAs.

Taking a Detailed Alcohol and Drug History

To facilitate the process of taking the initial alcohol and drug history, it is helpful to communicate to the patient that you are interested in the *use* of chemical substances and the patient's concerns about substances (rather than focusing on substance *abuse*). Focusing on substance *abuse* is likely to increase resistance in those patients who are reluctant to connect any of their current problems with their own substance use — wishing to see the parents' substance abuse as the primary source of current troubles. The patient who may have abused substances in the past, but who may not recognize this past substance use as abusive, may also be inclined to present a bland history if the emphasis is on *abuse*. It is thus important that a structured interview be carried out that actively enlists the patient in providing a detailed history of his *use* of all mood-altering substances.

One of the more neutral ways of obtaining this information is to have a check list or history questionnaire handy such as the one included in Appendix A. This makes it clear to the patient that you

---

*It should be noted that the ACOA groups discussed in this chapter are intended specifically for nonsubstance-abusing ACOAs. This is consistent with our view that ACOA groups should not be for currently active substance abusers or for patients still in early stages of recovery. The focus on parental abuse may not only distract from one's own focus on sobriety, but may, at times, serve as a rationale for continued drinking.

are asking questions that you ask of all of your patients (or all of your ACOAs, depending on how you present this information to the patient).

When asking about substance use, an important indicator that more exploration may be needed is the patient's categorical denial of *any* acquaintance with a given substance. For example, the patient may be asked, "Could you tell me something about your use of alcohol?" If she responds, "I never drink," the therapist should then inquire, "How long has this been the case? Have you ever made an exception?" (and other similar explorations). Similarly, the patient should be asked, "Could you tell me something about your use of opiates — codeine, percodan, morphine, etc."? If the patient says, "I've never used any of these," the therapist should then inquire, "How about when you've had surgery, teeth pulled, bad coughs, headaches, etc.?" Unless specifically questioned, patients may give categorically negative responses in order to move the interview on and to avoid this area of inquiry. And unless further inquiry is actually carried out, it is difficult to assess whether a minimal response is due to resistance or genuinely reflects minimal usage. Patients may also assume — unless specifically asked — that any drug that has been *prescribed* does not count and is therefore not worth mentioning. The neutral questionnaire format will help the interviewer to cover the full territory in a way that feels relatively unthreatening to the patient (particularly if the focus is on a detailed overview of *use*, not abuse).

If you have gathered enough data to suggest the possibility of an alcohol problem, the Michigan Alcoholism Screening Test (Hedlund & Vieweg, 1984; Selzer, 1971) may also be helpful. This questionnaire, which can be interviewer or self administered, includes 25 items covering social consequences of drinking, presence of addictive symptoms, interpersonal problems, and health problems associated with drinking. Items are differentially weighted and the weighted item scores are summed. A total MAST score of 5 or above is indicative of alcoholism, a score of 4 is considered suggestive of problems with alcohol. The MAST has been more extensively used than any other alcoholism screening device and has been shown to be a sensitive,reliable and valid measure (Selzer, Vinokur, & van Rooijen, 1975). Its only drawback is that it does not differentiate current from prior, but now resolved, alcohol-related problems. Accompanied by a good clinical interview, however, this differentiation should be relatively easy to make. (See Appendix B for a copy of the MAST and a scoring key.)

Special Problem: Information Delay Regarding Patient's Substance Abuse

Although, as indicated, careful assessment is an essential part of the preparatory experience prior to joining the long-term ACOA group, occasionally the patient may deny use of substances during the initial evaluation interviews, and his substance problems will come up only after he is already in a long-term group and feeling safe enough to talk about them. Because we feel that the most immediate alcohol-related situation needs to be addressed in its own right, at that point we would triage the patient to our out-patient substance-abuse track. For example, a young woman who had been in one of our ACOA groups for some months finally brought her own considerable substance-abuse problem to the attention of the group. At that point, we referred her to our five-week education and therapy sequence for substance abusers, and contracted with her to give up all substances. Since she was already very attached to her ACOA group, we allowed her to continue in that group. However, in addition, after completing the five-week education/therapy sequence in the substance track, we required that she join a long-term group for substance abusers.

Pregroup Preparation: Setting the Group Contract

It is important that the patient understand, before joining the group, what he can expect as a member and what will be expected of him. In our clinic, prior to beginning the five-week group experience, patients are given a handout by their intake interviewer that briefly describes the way our dynamically oriented therapy groups work and states specific ground rules (see Appendix C). More specifically, patients are told that a special feature of this kind of therapy group is that it provides a mirror of other important groups to which people belong and, as such, provides a setting in which to examine patterns of behavior with both in-dividuals and groups. They are also told that it provides a special setting in which new ways of relating can be tried out. The im-portance of intermember participation is emphasized as well as the therapist's role in facilitating this. Ground rules include: regular and timely attendance, payment for sessions missed without prior notice, timely payment of bills, and notification at least three weeks prior to terminating. Confidentiality is stressed, and mem-bers are told that they will be expected to talk about important issues in their lives that cause difficulty in relating to others or in living life fully, as well as about what is going on in the group itself as a better way of understanding their own interpersonal dynam-ics. Finally, in order to keep the group energy as much as possible within the group, patients are encouraged to keep outside-of-group contact to a minimum and are asked to discuss with the group any "relevant" discussions that come up outside.

When patients are referred to the long-term groups, a pre-group interview is held with the leader, and the ground rules are again reviewed. During the pregroup interview(s), the group lead-er also assesses whether the patient adequately understands the ground rules and will be able to behaviorally endorse them.

No matter how specific and detailed the initial treatment contract, even the most explicit ground rules will be understood differently by different members, and at different points in the group's history. Although the group ground rules that we use (see Appendix C) have been reworked a number of times to minimize ambiguity, misinterpretations by group members still occur. It is thus important in preparing the patients in the pregroup interview, and whenever the ground rules come up at later points in the life of the group, that the review of the ground rules takes place as a *process*, and not merely as an itemization of a list.

During the pregroup interview(s) it is also generally a good idea for the group leader to prepare the potential group member for the likelihood of resistance emerging at various points along the way — perhaps in the form of wishes not to attend on a given night, withdrawing from the group in silence, etc. Patients should be told that this is not uncommon and happens to most people at one point or another once they get into the work of therapy, but that what is most important is that the patient talk about these kinds of feelings, rather than acting on them. It is also helpful if leaders can anticipate with new group members, during the pregroup interview, the ways in which they are likely to resist or pull back that are familiar to them from other aspects of their lives. The therapist and patient may then agree that when these behaviors occur they will serve as signals that something important is going on that needs to be talked about in the group.

Simultaneous Membership in Other Groups*

Al-Anon and Group Therapy

A commonly encountered situation with groups of ACOAs is that many of the members will simultaneously be members of Al-Anon. In fact, for many, membership in Al-Anon may be the only kind of group treatment that they have experienced before joining a therapy group — an experience that is likely to have a strong influence on their expectations about group therapy.

It is thus important to underscore the ways in which the ground rules of Al-Anon and group therapy differ — namely, that membership in a therapy group carries with it the expectation that patients will be at the group every week and on time, will call in if for some reason they are unable to come, and will give advance notice to the group should they consider discontinuing membership. Although these ground rules are not unique to ACOA therapy groups, and would be stated as part of the initial treatment contract for any therapy group, it is particularly important that they be underscored at the time of the pregroup interview because they do differ substantially from the ground rules of Al-Anon. Other ways in which the therapy group may differ from Al-Anon should also be clarified. These include the therapy group's commitment to examining the group process itself, its focus on feelings and learning to communicate them more clearly, and its openness to exploring the past as well as the present with the goal of better integrating and understanding one's life experiences and feelings.

---

*Many of these issues have also been discussed with regard to group psychotherapy with alcoholic patients and their spouses in Vannicelli (1982, 1984).

Although patients will sometimes feel that there is conflict between their Al-Anon and group therapy experiences because the formats are so different, the therapist should be clear in his own mind that the two are not in any way mutually exclusive but, rather, serve different functions and provide support in distinct but complementary ways.

Education Task Group and Group Therapy

Not only are ACOAs likely to be members of Al-Anon while they are participating in a therapy group, but they will also often have had experience in a task-oriented ACOA education group. Like membership in Al-Anon, participation in groups that have a substantially didactic component carries with it a prescribed set of expectations and ground rules that differ from the ground rules of a therapy group. It is thus helpful in the pregroup interview to prepare new members by differentiating group therapy not only from Al-Anon but also from an education group. The therapist may say directly, "The purpose of this group is not so much to give you answers and provide information, but more to help you explore and better understand feelings and situations that you find difficult to manage, and to better understand where you fit in with the difficulties that you experience."

This chapter has examined some of the issues that the group leader must consider in deciding whether or not to begin an ACOA therapy group, how to set it up, and procedures for selecting and preparing the members. Once the decision is made to begin a group, the leader needs to decide on the group's size and composition, whether members will be simultaneously in individual therapy with the leader, and whether the group will be open-ended or time-limited. In addition, procedures need to be established for selecting and prescreening members and for preparing members during the pregroup interview about what they can expect from the group, as well as what will be expected of them. The next chapter considers some of the issues that the leader must deal with when he actually assembles the members and begins the group.

4
Beginning the Group

The group leader's initial task is to help the group bond so that group members will feel safe in assuming a self-reflective pose while interacting with one another in the immediate present. Although, there is an inherent movement toward bonding in ACOA groups (which will be discussed further in Chapter 5), there are a number of things that leaders can do to help facilitate and enhance initial group bonding.

Preparing the Room

It is the therapist's responsibility to provide an appropriate environment for the group — one that is pleasant, relatively free of outside noise and distractions, and is spatially arranged to allow for maximal intermember contact. The latter is too often not adequately attended to. It is most important that the room space be adequate to allow for a circle to be formed, and that before the meeting leaders position chairs so that all members will have easy visual access to one another. A group can get off to a shaky start when some members have difficulty making contact with one another visually, and are too inhibited (as many members are, initially) to move their chairs in such a way as to regain contact. As a leader, if I find myself in such a situation — that is, where for some reason my view of a given patient is blocked, I actively squirm and noticeably move my chair back and forth, making as many adjustments as necessary. My behavior thus signals that I want to maximize my ability to see *everyone*.

Arrangements where some of the patients are side by side (for example, along a couch), where the chairs are of different heights, or where members' views of one another are obstructed by other pieces of furniture (lamps, tables, etc.) are less than ideal and should be avoided.

The Initial Meeting: Helping Members Begin

Although all group members, presumably through the course of their pregroup meeting(s), will have become familiar with the group ground rules (the contract) and will have had an opportunity to examine their goals for work in the group, it is often helpful during the first meeting for members to have a chance to collectively reiterate the group ground rules and to share with one another what it is they are hoping to work on in the group.

Since for some members the ACOA group will be their first group therapy experience (or perhaps their first therapy experience), it is to be expected that some will have "cold feet." A number of strategies may be useful in helping members to deal with initial awkwardness and hesitancy about how to proceed. For example, when group silences occur, leaders may intervene more directly by asking, "What makes it hard to begin?" or, "What makes it hard for the group to continue?" In addition, individual patients who are silent during much of the initial session may need special attention. Leaders may draw in such members initially by commenting, "Some people seem to be finding it difficult to enter," and wondering, "What may make it difficult?" Often patients will respond with something like, "I'm not sure what to say . . . don't know where to begin. I just feel anxious and confused." The therapist might help such a patient by pointing out that his earnest self-disclosure (reflected in his faltering comment) is just what is needed for the group to be able to begin (Alpert, 1988). The leader might say, "Joe, what you're doing right now is just what needs to happen in a group like this. You are sharing some of your feelings in the present moment about what it's like to be here and your uncertainty about the whole thing." Thus, the patient is being told that he *does* know what to do and is, in fact, doing it.

Since the hope is that all group members will feel at least some connection to the group by the end of the first session, specific strategies may also be useful for promoting group cohesion. As Alpert (1988) suggests, it is important for each group member "to make a connection with at least one other member." This kind of bonding can be facilitated by the leader's active efforts to "make links whenever possible" between members — for example, by underlining similarities among group members (p. 1). Thus, the leaders may say, "It seems that Sue and Bob, and perhaps others in here as well, are struggling with very similar problems with their anger." Occasionally, particularly in the initial sessions, group members may present what appears to be a united front *against* perceiving themselves to be similar to one another — each claiming, for example, how "unique and different" his situation is. Even here, a sense of commonality can be created by the leader who may comment, "This sense of being different in some important way is something that you all have in common."

Other strategies that may be helpful initially in building cohesion are also described by Alpert (1988): (1) encouraging thoughts about the group between sessions, for example, by asking members to share thoughts that they have had about the group as a whole or about individual members during the week that has intervened since the last meeting; and (2) "underlining subtle positive feelings about the group that are not yet fully apparent" — a technique that Alpert refers to as "pump priming for positive group feeling" (p. 2). The group leader can prime the pump in this way by turning a chorus of complaints about "how hard it was to get here tonight" into a statement of the group's emerging value for its members. Thus, the leader may say, "It has taken some real effort for each of you to get here tonight, yet each of you has made a point of doing so — an indication, perhaps, of some of the hopeful feelings that are beginning to develop."

Providing Appropriate "Boundaries" around the Group Time

Whenever possible, it is preferable if the leaders can be present both to "open" and to "close" the group. Thus, ideally, leaders will already be in the room and will have had an opportunity to arrange the chairs (and when co-leading, to confer with one another) prior to the group's beginning. Keeping the group-room door closed until the time the group begins and then opening it promptly at the starting time provides an even cleaner boundary, since patients do not then trickle in and begin small talk with one another, or with the leaders, prior to the official beginning of the group. Less desirable, though sometimes unavoidable, is the situation in which the group-room door is simply left open and members enter as they arrive, the leader joining them at the designated starting time. Although the leader's arrival thus signals the beginning of the group, this model has the disadvantage that the leader often feels that he has "interrupted something" that is already taking place.

Tidy boundaries around closing the group are equally important. Ideally, leaders will remain in the group room until the last member exits. When leaders must hasten to get away, leaving members to remain in the group room, the boundaries are less clear. (I have been told that some groups continue, without their leaders, for prolonged sessions after the close of the official group). Although it may be true that group members do something somewhat similar in the lobby when they all exit together, the clear boundary around the official group space provides a safer, cleaner containing environment.

If a group is already in place in which boundaries are less clear cut than the leader would prefer, remediation may be possible, even if the group has been in existence for some time. For example, in one of our clinic groups in which leaders had other obligations just prior to the group, they had developed the habit of setting up the group room in advance and then going off to their other responsibilities on the hospital campus. They would then return just before the group was scheduled to begin, but often felt, upon their arrival, that they were interrupting something that was already in process. They decided to modify this situation by telling group members that in the future, the room would be kept locked until the leaders arrived, and that members should wait in the waiting room until the group's designated starting time. In another group, where leaders needed to leave promptly at the end of the group, and the group members often lingered on for lengthy postgroup sessions, the leaders similarly informed the group that in the future they would need to lock up the group room upon their departure. Thus, when the group ended, leaders stood at the door, keys in hand, until the last member exited.

Clear boundaries around the time frame of the group are also important with regard to members' arrivals and departures. A clear message should be given that members are expected to arrive on time and to remain for the *entire session*. There should be a clearly stated expectation that, regardless of how heated the group process may get, group members will remain in the room and talk about their feelings.

Maintaining the Boundaries of the Group: Intermember Interactions

The boundaries of the group will also be strengthened by clearly articulating the following ground rules: members are expected to attend regularly, to hold confidential what other members share, and to minimize outside-of-group contact.* With regard to the latter, it is important that members have a shared understanding that although it is likely that members may see one another at Al-Anon meetings or at Al-Anon/ACOA support groups, it is desirable to keep as much of the group energy as possible within the group. As Rutan and Stone (1984) indicate,

> The fundamental use of the group is for therapeutic, not social, purposes, and in the long run the two are mutually exclusive. (Thus) . . . it is more therapeutically profitable to discourage extragroup socializing, since doing so reduces the variables affecting group behavior and increases the likelihood of spontaneous revelation of affects in the group. (p. 110)

Thus, patients should be encouraged to keep outside-of-group contact to a minimum, and also to discuss with the group any "relevant" content that comes up outside. Although the word "relevant" is somewhat vague, and different members will surely interpret it in different ways, there should be a shared understand-

---

*These issues are also elaborated with regard to the group treatment of alcoholic patients in Vannicelli (1982).

ing that if the outside-of-group contact exceeds the usual socializing in the waiting room or at Al-Anon meetings, it should be discussed with the group. It is sometimes helpful to give concrete examples — for instance, if two group members find themselves socializing extensively or having a "special" liaison; or if two group members find themselves discussing, even briefly, their feelings about other members, the leader, or the group itself. Discussion of these examples should help clarify that important relationships that takes place outside and are not discussed with the group rob the group as a whole of the opportunity to explore these matters and rob the individuals involved of the opportunity to get valuable feedback from other members. Equally important, the outside-of-group business that does not get talked about within the group takes on the character of "special secrets," the existence of which runs counter to the group's shared goal of mutual openness and trust.

In the initial phases of the group, and also at times of stress in the group, members may move toward deliberately increasing the "social" aspect of the group. Although members may feel that this may help them to feel "closer" to one another, it also generally serves to dilute the intensity of the group work by creating a "safe" friendship network. Thus, group members may openly discuss in the group the possibility of social gatherings at one another's homes, postgroup pizza-get-togethers, etc. Although our clinic group ground rules do not forbid this activity, our group leaders use a number of strategies to help shape the norms about minimal outside-of-group contact. First, when actual socializing or the wish to socialize comes up, leaders take an actively exploratory attitude about it, asking, "What does it mean to group members to have these socializing opportunities?" "How do members imagine that the group might be different were the socializing *not* to take place?" "What functions do members imagine that the socializing might serve for the group itself?" Leaders may also create an expectation that, once the group is fully under way and functioning at its highest potential as a therapy group, the socializing or the wish for socializing will decrease. Leaders might say something such as, "At this point, there seems to be a feeling that members cannot get enough from one another during our one-and-a-half hour weekly meetings and that for members needs to be adequately met, more time, different formats, etc. are needed. I have a hunch, however, that as we get to know one another better and really get down to the work that group members came for, the outside-of-group contact will decrease."

Shaping Group Norms with Forecasts and Hunches

At times, particularly early in the history of the group, it may be useful for the leader to make deliberate efforts to shape group norms concerning effective behavior that will promote the work of the group. One of my favorite shaping strategies (briefly illustrated in the previous section) is to make use of positive forecasts or "hunches." For example, to a group member who is reluctant to talk about a particularly painful area, the group leader might say, "I have a hunch that this is something you will feel more comfortable talking about as you know people in here better." Or, the therapist may "predict" a change in group behavior based on her knowledge of the way that groups develop. For example, in response to group members' outside-of-group contacts, the leader might comment, "In groups such as ours, outside-of-group contact generally diminishes as group members feel more comfortable with one another and more ready to begin to know one another in a different, more therapeutic kind of way." Group leaders may also encourage the development of transference (and group members' willingness to discuss transference feelings) with forecasts such as, "I'd expect that as we work together members will come to have a variety of feelings about other members, as well as about the leaders, and will find it helpful to talk about these feelings."

Negative behaviors, too, can be commented on and "shaped" by the use of positive forecasts. For example, to the patient who repeatedly protests in any heated situation that he "has no feelings," a leader might posit, "I have a hunch that you, like all of us in here, have many different kinds of feelings and that, with time, we will come to understand more about them." Or, to the patient who rambles on and on with extensive details, the leader might predict, "I have a hunch that as you feel more understood in here, you will feel less pressured to provide us with quite so much detail when you explain what is going on for you." Many behaviors related to ground rules can similarly be "shaped" by forecasting positive performance in the future. For example, regarding lateness and absenteeism, a leader might comment, "I have a hunch that as members come to know that they can count on others to be here for them, greater efforts will be made to make this the very highest priority on Tuesday nights."

Basically, positive forecasts underscore that as group members come to have more positive feelings about the group (more trust, greater comfort, etc.) and that as the group gets down to work, certain kinds of positive or proactive behaviors are more likely to occur, and behaviors that get in the way of group growth will decrease. Such leader comments are useful, not only because they promote positive expectations and an aura of optimism, but also because they provide explicit guideposts that help the group and individual members to judge when progress is being made.

This chapter has examined several ways in which the leader sets the stage for the group members to bond and begin working together. The leader accomplishes this by: providing an appropriate setting for the group, helping members to get started, and providing adequate boundaries around the group. The next chapter deals with group themes that emerge as the group develops.

5
Special Issues and Themes

There are a number of themes and issues which, while not unique to psychodynamically oriented groups with ACOAs, do seem to occur more frequently in these groups and may at times take on somewhat greater importance. However, before discussing these special themes, it is important to emphasize that the group work that we do with ACOA patients is, for the most part, very similar to the work we do with other populations in our clinic and with other generic psychiatric outpatient populations. This is consistent with our view of ACOAs as a diagnostically heterogeneous group of patients who vary considerably in terms of symptoms, presenting issues, and level of functioning. As Hibbard (1987) clearly states,

> Character disorders and the kinds of underlying pathology we are mentioning are not unique or specific to ACAs.* There is nothing uniquely discernible, no newly discovered nosological entity in this treatment population. To the contrary, it is by applying familiar developmental analytical concepts and broadly accepted assessment tools that ACAs can be empathically understood. (p. 780)

The themes and problems that emerge in ACOA groups occur in all dynamically oriented therapy groups. Moreover, an ACOA who is placed in a group that is not specifically designed for ACOAs (e.g., a group of substance abusers or a group for family members — or even in a generic outpatient group) is still likely to enact many of these same themes. What differentiates the ACOA group is not the presence of these themes, but, rather, the frequen-

---

*ACA is another frequent abbreviation for Adult Children of Alcoholics.

cy with which they occur, the enthusiasm with which they may be embraced, and the group's tenacity in holding onto them.

As has been indicated, part of the glue for initial and continued bonding in ACOA groups is the common presenting issue regarding the ACOA identity. This homogeneity around the presenting issue continues to create greater intensity within the group than is often true of more heterogeneous groups because there is less diffusion of focus. In heterogeneous therapy groups, some patients present around issues with parents, others around dysfunctional behavior in the workplace, others present with feelings that have been stirred up over the loss of a lover or spouse, and others with diffuse anxiety or depression. Moreover, members enter at different stages of awareness regarding the importance of past family experiences in understanding their current presenting issues. It sometimes takes months — even years — for patients to link up their present difficulties to issues in their families of origin (and there is often considerable resistance to doing this). The diversity among members provides more ready diversion and distraction from the intense family-of-origin and transference issues that are ultimately part of any therapy group. In contrast, in the ACOA group all members come with the knowledge that their work involves rethinking issues regarding their past relationships with their families of origin and how these issues relate to the present. Although members may vary considerably in terms of level of sophistication and clinical awareness, the family is a more ready focus for the overt content of the group, and family transference is more readily enacted.

Thus, the themes that will be described in the following material are likely to take on special meaning in ACOA groups because they recapture the family dynamics of *several* members — with a greater number of group members lending themselves to the group enactments that emerge (and fewer members left to provide observing ego). It is thus especially important that the leader is prepared for these themes, understands what is going on, and is able to provide a healthy observing ego, when necessary.

With this caveat about the nonexclusiveness of these themes, this chapter will now explore some of the more common themes that are likely to emerge in an ACOA group. As will be readily noted, most of the themes relate in one way or another to the powerful "family dynamic" that gets played out through the course of the therapy.

The powerful family transference that develops (which occurs, of course, in all dynamically oriented therapy groups) is particularly potent in these groups for a number of reasons. First, many ACOAs fear, as they first enter treatment, that in talking about family "secrets" they are in some way abandoning or betraying their families of origin (Beletsis & Brown, 1981). This is often further complicated by a long-standing (and forbidden) wish to be able to separate emotionally (or even physically) from their families. There are thus conflicting feelings involving betrayal and abandonment, as well as a healthy wish to separate. As one patient put it (Beletsis & Brown, 1981),

> I feel like I'm involved in a minuet, with intricate and specific dance steps. If I want to step out or do a different step the whole family is threatened and I will never get back in. (p. 23)

The fear that, by entering therapy and making changes, the ACOA will be abandoning (or will be abandoned by) the family of origin makes the entry into a new "family" (the group) an even more powerfully loaded venture. As Brown (1988) suggests, transference thus develops quickly and often intensely, as members embrace the new family that at least in fantasy, will replace the one they are leaving behind. Along with this, the group leaders also become powerful transference figures — and often, initially, highly idealized. There is an understandable hope and wish that the leaders will provide the good (perhaps perfect) parenting that was absent in childhood, and that the group will be the close and supportive family long yearned for. This conscious idealization of the family group tends to be even more prominent than in more heterogeneous therapy groups — in part because it is more likely to meet a shared and salient need of many of the members.

However, the power of the positive idealization (the initial cement of the group) also carries with it the seeds of its obverse — negative transference and feelings of intense disappointment. In other words, the powerful, initial family wishes and fantasies that create the rapid bonding lead to greater initial investment. However, along with this there may also be greater intensity of negative feelings, including tremendous fear of disappointment — and often actual disappointment. As we shall see, this powerful initial chemistry relates substantially to most of the themes that follow.

Flight from the Group (The Wish to Leave Prematurely)

The wish to leave an ACOA group is an ever-present theme, and threats to leave or run away are frequently expressed, either in terms of wishes to flee from the session or to terminate from the group. The fantasied solutions of the past ("escape" from the pain and conflict) are thus reenacted in the ACOA group over and over again as conflict is encountered and as tension levels rise. Because there was no doubt a time for many ACOAs when the fantasy of running away was all that sustained them, it is not surprising that group members continue to think about it (and even attempt to enact it) as a solution in the new family group as well. It is often useful for leaders to help group members understand that their wish represents a fantasied solution of the past, but that it is not a solution that will help them in dealing effectively with the current "family" (the therapy group); and that while things may feel extremely intense and precarious, this is not in fact the old family but a new one in which alternative, constructive options to fleeing are available. It may also be useful to help group members understand, more generally, about the intense "family glue" that gets aroused in these groups, along with the fears of disappointment, and how this chemistry stirs up old impulses and wishes to flee.

It should also be noted that the wish to flee, in addition to being a familiar solution to old family conflicts and stresses, may also emerge because of new feelings that are being stirred up. Even the "positive" feelings regarding the "perfect" parents and the wonderful, close family can be powerfully frightening for those members who have had little experience regulating closeness and intimacy.

Finding (and Removing) the Identified Family Problem

Although scapegoating may occur in any group, ACOA groups are often especially inclined to pick "an identified patient" (IP), whom the group may first "try to cure," ultimately decide is "too sick," and finally attempt to extrude. As in most instances of scapegoating, the chosen IP complies in some way, as he or she shares the group fantasy and lends himself to its enactment. In this instance, the collective myth is that the family will finally be restored to happiness when the "problem" is removed. In other words, the group enacts the cherished fantasy of childhood that the idealized family will finally occur if the troubled (alcoholic) member is gone. In fact, the group may move from one patient to another, attempting to discover "who is the sickest," in order to target the identified patient so that the group can either cure or extrude him and thereby restore the health of the family.

The Search for a Rescuer

Closely related to the group's search for the "problem" patient is the search for a grand and powerful figure who will "come to the rescue." While initially this wish may be projected onto the group leaders in the form of idealized transference, as the group moves on (and particularly as the group leaders come to be viewed with more ambivalence) the group may look for a "rescuer" among themselves. The patient who is assigned this role (and who, often, all too willingly complies) may then become as rigidly stuck in this position as the identified patient may become in his.

It falls to the group leaders in both instances (with the scapegoated "identified patient" and the assigned "hero") to help the group understand its need to have these roles filled, and also to understand the ways in which the designated actors comply. In the case of scapegoating, it is sometimes helpful for the leader to ask if the identified patient might in some way be "serving a function for the group." If the group has difficulty responding, the leader may help further by proposing some possible suggestions such as, "I have a hunch that the group's view of Sam as 'the sick one' — perhaps too sick for this group — might be helpful to the group in recreating some old, familiar patterns. I wonder if it's possible that the group's wish to cure him or get rid of him might feel like a solution that could be understood from the past."

Similar questions to the group about the role of the rescuer might be as follows: "It seems as if the group has a powerful wish to see Susan as the 'rescuer' in here. I wonder if Susan's portrayal of herself as so much healthier than the other group members, and the group's readiness to buy this, might serve some function for the group." After exploring these questions, the leaders may again share their hunches about the possibility that the group is enacting something in the present that might have seemed like a solution from the past. And again, although the entire group's involvement in the enactment will be important, the particular individual's willingness (and wish) to play a particular role should also be explored.

Rigid Role Assignments

In both of the themes illustrated above (scapegoat and rescuer), it is clear that in these groups members may find themselves solidly entrenched in specific, relatively limited roles, with the collusion and support of the group. Although, to some extent, this dynamic is possible in all psychodynamically oriented therapy groups, it may be exaggerated in these groups because dysfunctional families may be particularly likely to develop stereotyped and rigid roles that keep the family system in balance. A series of research studies (Davis et al., 1974; Steinglass, 1979; Steinglass et al., 1977) have documented that alcoholic families display a more rigid interactional style than is the case with nonalcoholic families, and that family members tend to act in more rigidly coordinated patterns, particularly during alcohol-free periods. Although there is no empirical validation to date for the particular *kinds* of roles that individuals may play, there is some research that suggests, at least, a certain level of role constriction and stereotypy of response — perhaps due in part to a need to increase predictability in an arena in which this is frequently lacking. The quest for predictability may manifest itself similarly in the ACOA group, where again people may fall into predictable roles with regard to one another and with regard to the group. For example:

> Sue was seen as the helper and "healthy member" of the group. Because of the group's need for her to fill this role, as well as her

own need to preserve it, certain other work was avoided. It was very slow work for Sue and the group to see her stance as a protective maneuver. The group (spearheaded initially by the leaders) slowly chipped away at her "helper" role and her need (as well as the group's) to see herself as healthier than the rest and as a symbol of the one who had "made it" by leaving a sick family behind. The therapist began addressing this by asking, "How would it be for you, Sue, if you weren't in fact the healthiest member here and 'way beyond' the rest of the group? What would it be like for you if you were very much like and with the other members?" (The leader was chipping away at Sue's fears of intimacy — shielded by her "I am distant because I am superior" stance.)

Hanging On

Although less common than the theme of flight, another theme that reenacts a part of the old family drama is tenacious "hanging on." Some patients, even after they have finished the work they came for, find that they cannot leave. Termination dates are repeatedly set, and as they approach, new concerns and issues emerge. While sometimes there is, indeed, more work to be done (and the work of termination involves refocusing patients in such a way that it becomes clear that there is more to do) it is also important to pay attention to patients who cannot leave because of an inability to let go.

For such patients, many of whom lived much of their childhoods in hopeful anticipation that things might one day get better, hanging on has become a dysfunctional solution. They continue to live with the persistent feeling that if they hang on a little longer, the longed-for "pearl" will finally be delivered. They are unable to leave the group because they cling to the old hope and fantasy that with a little more time and a little more effort, a little more will be forthcoming. Such patients have difficulty separating from the group (and often separating from inappropriate people in their lives outside of the group) because they cannot let go of the hope that, with steadfast persistence, Cinderella's wish (the yearned-for connection, closeness, and caring) will finally come true. Such patients live with the fantasy, which they reenact over and over in their lives, that the people that they love will one day return the caring measure-for-measure; and that if they just hang in long enough and do enough, they will finally get what they have held out for.

These patients need to understand that these fantasies, while offering great "staying power," often prevent them from getting their needs met from other more appropriate sources. People, including group members and group leaders, have their limits. The fantasy of what one "should have gotten" and is still holding out for may not be in keeping with what is realistically available. To help such patients terminate from the group, it is often necessary to help them understand the real limitations that existed in past relationships, and the groups' limitations as well.

> *Miss Stayer attempted to terminate from her group three times (each time with three-months notice and considerable processing), only to decide in the end that she was not ready to leave. Before she finally successfully terminated, it was necessary for her to work through the hard-to-relinquish fantasy that all mothers, including her own, really do love their children, and if the child would only come up with the right formula, she would be the recipient of that love. In her final phase of work with the group, Miss Stayer came to understand her mother's limitations: she had conceived Miss Stayer during an alcoholic blackout and was psychologically unprepared for motherhood; she resented her daughter's arrival, which required that she drop out of high school; and throughout her daughter's developing years, she experienced her child's thriving not only to be occurring at the cost of her own education and development, but also as an insulting and injurious contrast (experienced competitively) with her own failure. Through her work in the group, Miss Stayer came to understand that her alcoholic mother had given what she could (sadly, often amounting to very little), and that there were no more solutions, in the past or in the present, that could change what her mother could give. She finally accepted that she had gotten what she could from her mother. Although she had gotten a great deal from the group (and could readily acknowledge this), she finally was also able to give up the fantasy that if she hung in a little longer she could get even a little more.*

For many patients, the myth that "all mothers love their children," leads not only to inappropriate hanging on but also to repetitive poor choices in love objects. The yearning to get from "mother stand-ins" the yearned-for approval and affection that mother was unable to give is often replayed over and over with future significant others, as the patient continues to chose love objects who can never fully acknowledge love nor love back in return.* Such patients continue, often throughout repeated relationships, to "turn somersaults" in order to get what seems not to be forthcoming.

Negative Self-View to Preserve Parental "Goodness"

Early and unmet needs for love and support may lead not only to dysfunctional relationships, but also to dysfunctional hanging on to a negative self-identity. The need to believe that parents are "good" and "loving" is basic to a child's sense of safety and security. When reality challenges this basic assumption, the child from a dysfunctional family alters beliefs about *himself* to protect parental goodness and integrity (Brown, 1988; Wood, 1987). Simply stated, if a child perceives himself as "bad" he justifies parental neglect and even abuse by his otherwise "good" parents. As Brown (1988) states

> The child experiences the absence or loss of parental attention as a *response to* something bad about the child . . . (thus providing) an illusion of security because it leaves the parents intact as available and caring figures and places the responsibility for problems on the child. (p. 132)

Wood (1987), succinctly summarizing the thinking of the British object relation's theorists (Fairbairn, 1943/1981; Guntrip, 1969; Winnicott, 1955/1975), adds to our understanding of this important dynamic:

> . . . when children cannot build satisfying relations with their parents — because the parents are abusive, neglectful, or both — the children try to achieve a sense of control over their terrifying predicament by internalizing those aspects of the parents that seem most frightening and destructive. . . . These psychic maneuvers permit children to maintain an illusory sense of control over a threatening situation, but be-

---

*This dynamic may also occur when the father has been the unloving parent.

cause the bad objects are installed in the psyche and become part of the self, they have devastating effects on self-esteem. (p. 29)

Citing Fairbairn (1943/1981), she concludes:

. . . "bad relationships with objects" who are crucial to one's survival are physically intolerable for children . . . (thus) they cope by 'taking the burden of badness' into themselves. . . . This has the agreeable effect of creating a secure, 'good' outer field, but produces a hellish condition inside the child.
As Fairbairn put it, the feeling of "outer security is . . . purchased at the price of inner security . . . [and the] ego is henceforth left at the mercy of a band of internal fifth columnists or persecutors." (p. 55)

> *Clinical Example: A group member poignantly described his highly critical mother who laughed at him unmercifully and rarely held or soothed him. All normal feelings were ridiculed as "the reactions of a supersensitive child," leaving the patient to feel inadequate and abnormal. When this young man realized, through the course of his group work, that his mother had been ridiculing him for what amounted to normal behavior, he experienced tremendous pain. In response to the leader's comment, "It seems as if you never got the feedback that you needed, that you were, in fact, quite normal," he burst out, "I don't want information that I was 'normal' — I want to lock it up so that I can love my mother." At that moment, the patient was experiencing powerfully conflictual wishes. On the one hand, he wished to see himself as normal — in which case he would have to see his mother as bad; while on the other, he wished to maintain his loving feelings about his mother which could be done only by perceiving himself as abnormal or bad.*

The ACOA Label

For many ACOAs, another aspect of negative self-identity may include the ACOA label itself. Although identification of oneself as an ACOA has many positive aspects, particularly in terms of feeling that one's problems can be understood and remediated, overattachment to one's "ACOAness" may ultimately impair growth by perpetuating a negative self-view. As one group member put it when he began to form healthier relations with peers, "I no longer wish to have so much of my world view focused on my ACOAness."

As discussed earlier, in the process of identity formation, the child takes into himself important aspects of the intimate world with which he interacts. Negative as well as positive aspects of the child's world are thus incorporated into his picture of himself. As described, through this process some of the most negative aspects of the child's interpersonal environment may be transmuted into something less damaging by making certain negative assumptions about the "self." Thus, a small child, who needs to feel that his world is safe and that his caretakers are basically good, may take in the "bad" of the parents into his picture of himself ("I am the bad one"), thereby cleansing the parents and leaving them the good, caring objects that he so desperately needs. Through this kind of mechanism we understand how the ACOA, attempting in a sense "to spare his parents" and keep them as "good" as possible, in exchange, takes on a bad or negative picture of himself. These bad parts become an important part of the identity of the ACOA. It is thus important to keep in mind that an overly salient identity as an ACOA may reflect not a healthy adaptation but, rather, a need to cling to a bad view of oneself in order to keep the world in balance.

A recent ad in the "personals" section of *Boston Magazine* captures the salience of an ACOA identity for this particular individual. It began: "DWF 46 FRIEND OF BILL W's ACOA, nonsmoker, loves humor. . . ." This ad, I think, reflects the enormous importance of the ACOA identity to this individual and her wish to preserve it in subsequent relationships with significant others. She was putting out a sign, unconsciously inviting those who would pair with her "defective" part (and continue to reinforce it) to join her in a relationship.

The goal of group therapy is to put the ACOA identity in its proper perspective. That one's parents were alcoholic is a to-be-accepted fact. The ACOA's picture of himself will always involve this fact, and through the course of therapy it will help explain many aspects of the patient's past. Brown (1988) indicates that for many ACOAs ". . . the most significant change begins with the acquisition of the identity ACA" — the first step in "making real the past" (p. 291). Yet ideally, with successful therapy, and the emergence of a more positive and more integrated self, the centrality of the ACOA identity will recede.

The Myth of Equality

Another group theme frequently played out in ACOA groups is the "myth of equality." This myth represents a fantasy about the kind of equality that occurs in the "ideal" family in which all (group members) are equal and all are "winners." The myth is that mother and father (and the group leaders) feel exactly the same about each of them. To the extent that a group perpetuates this myth (denying, rather than examining, differences in leader behavior with different members), the group stalemates important work around competition, jealousy, and envy.

In one group, when members continued to talk about the leaders' "equal feelings toward all members" and "no apparent favorites," leaders challenged this idea with comments such as, "The myth of absolute equality in here seems to be very important to the group. What would it be like to imagine that the leaders had different feelings, expectations, and attitudes about different members?" The leaders also began to help members examine status differences and potential rivalries in the group by commenting, "Perhaps in some ways, some members are more equal than others."

The myth of equality, particularly in beginning groups, may also be reflected by an overly concrete view about division of time and attention in the group. Comments are frequent such as, "I've taken more than my share of the time tonight and Sam hasn't gotten his turn." Or, "I did all the talking last week, so I've gotten more than my share for awhile." Invariably, these assumptions falsely equate talking with "getting" and listening with "giving." When such a view is taken to its concrete and logical extreme, it would imply that with eight members in a 90-minute group each member, if all is going as it should be would get to talk approximately 11 minutes — that this is his time to "get" and that during the remaining 79 minutes members are either "giving" or are simply "on hold." Such myths clearly need to be challenged since they belie the dynamic interplay that makes group therapy so effective. As leaders, we are clearly aware that group members often get as much (or more) by listening as by talking, and that they often *give* more when talking than when listening.

It is useful for leaders to undercut assumptions of equal

division of time with statements such as the following: "This group seems to have the notion* that members 'get' in here only when they are talking and 'give' only when they are listening." Depending on what the group does with such a statement, group members might then be asked where such a notion might come from. A few clinical examples will illustrate how this myth can get played out in the group.

> In one group, the issue of "who is entitled to what" (translated into concerns about apportionment of time) took an amusing turn when the most recent member of the group expressed relief about the anticipated arrival of an even newer member the next week. When the new member appeared, she greeted him warmly and laughingly passed the "new-member baton." Discussions of what it had meant to her to be the newest member revealed that she felt that up until now she was entitled to "the smallest piece of the pie." When asked if she were allowed to do the serving how the pie would now be cut up, she pointed to the new member and said, "He'll just get a tiny sliver — just kidding."
>
> The idea of equal time, carried to its logical extreme, was described by a new member entering another group. In this member's former "group," members lined their chairs up in a row, meeting after meeting, and talked in turn based on their sitting position. This structured "equal" format, while initially perhaps feeling "safer" to group members, successfully undermined the dynamic interactional elements of group life so essential to its effective functioning.

Resistance to "Taking a Look" at What's Going On

Because children who grow up in dysfunctional families often get messages from their parents that seem to invalidate the child's perception that something is wrong, a coping strategy is sometimes developed of "not seeing" what's happening. Children from alcoholic families who confront their parents about drinking problems may be told that there is "no problem" or they may even be given the impression that they are "bad" for noticing. Thus, for many ACOAs, the experience of feeling uncomfortable about

---

*I sometimes use the word "notion" to suggest that an idea or assumption is worth further examining, and may not be as true as it first appears.

what's going on, but not feeling that they have either permission to really look at it or to voice their concerns, may be a common experience. Sometimes this will become apparent in the group when members have difficulty actually looking at one another or at the therapists; at other times it may become apparent when an individual group member or the group as a whole appears to have difficulty taking a real look at what's going on in the group itself. At such times, it may be helpful for group leaders to suggest to the group that "members seem to feel that in some ways they do not have permission to look or to really 'see' what's happening," and to suggest that this might be something that the group might want to take a better look at. Members, through the process of their group work, thus may have an opportunity, for the first time, to go back and take a look at their past experiences and to see them as they really were. At the same time they have an opportunity in the group to learn to look at how things really are in the present and to trust their perceptions of reality.

> My eyes filled when one of our oldest members was working on his termination and tenderly reviewing his course in the group and how much he had changed. Although most of the group was clearly engaged in the sweet sadness of the feelings that he was sharing, one of our newer members seemed very much disengaged from the process, while repeatedly taking quick little side glances at me. When I inquired about what was going on for her, she said, "I don't know. I guess I was sort of interested in your face." I asked what it was that she saw, and she responded, "I don't know exactly; you seem to be having some feelings, but I felt as if I wasn't supposed to notice — and that I certainly wasn't supposed to look." After helping her to describe what she did, in fact, "see" in my face, I said, "I have a hunch that you and perhaps others in the group, as well, often felt in the past as if you didn't really have permission to 'see what was going on.' In here we have a unique opportunity to work on that."

Fear of Losing Control or "Becoming Unglued" (Riskiness of Opening Up in the Group)

For many ACOAs, *not* talking about certain important emotions and experiences has become a norm, along with not seeing important things. Along with this, ideas about the self may have developed such that keeping things in is equated with keeping things "in order" and keeping oneself together. Thus, in the initial phases of ACOA groups, fears about "opening up," present in all new therapy groups, may be accompanied by fantasies of being overwhelmed or of coming "unglued." Thus, in early stages of group life, concerns about keeping things "in order" and "under control" may lead group members to press for closure around group rules, norms for appropriate behavior, and, in particular, the appropriate amount to reveal about oneself.

As Brown and Beletsis (1986) suggest, group members often equate strong feelings (i.e., feeling too happy, too sad, too angry, or revealing too much of any of these) with being out of control and being drunk. Not only may a member feel out of control when feeling that he or she is "revealing too much," but other members may have similar reactions based on their own low tolerance for the sustained emotional reactions of others. Thus, particularly in early stages of group life, when one member becomes emotional in describing a current problem (or feelings about another group member), other group members may act quickly to control or limit the expression of feelings. Group leaders can help the group with this, not only by modeling tolerance for expression of feeling, but more specifically, by helping members to appreciate that the group is a safe, "contained" place where feelings can be expressed. When the group attempts to abort the expression of feelings, leaders may comment, "It seems that the group is having trouble listening to Stephanie's anger. Perhaps there is a feeling that if we don't stop her, things will get out of control. But I wonder how we will come to understand what she is feeling if we are unable to let her share what's going on."

Other attempts to abort feelings may come, not from the group, but from the member who is feeling acute pain and is reluctant to get in touch with it. For such patients there may be a fear that if they give word to the pain of their past, they may "cry forever." In this instance, the group leader might help patients to articulate their concern while also gently challenging this idea. To the patient who responds, "If I start to open up, I might cry forever," the group leader might ask, "Did that ever happen?" Patients often respond with surprise to this question, since, of course, to some extent tears and sadness are always self-limiting. When the patient responds, "No, but I did cry for a long time," the therapist might ask, "How were you able to stop?" (thus focusing on the self-limiting mechanisms inherent in the patient). That one can learn ways of managing intense feelings, and that a situation that seems to feel a little out of control will not necessarily lead to total chaos and destruction, are important lessons for a group member who has lived in a dysfunctional family, where periods of being out of control frequently reached an intolerable pitch.

For some members of ACOA groups, the fear of "coming unglued" (associated, perhaps, with being hospitalized) may be a very real one. With such patients, the leaders can also focus on the patients' adaptive strengths while at the same time acknowledging the intense fears by saying something like, "I suspect that these fears of 'coming unglued' have been with you for a long time, and that alongside of these you've also developed ways of taking care of yourself. Perhaps at this moment you, as well as other group members, are having trouble remembering the ways in which you have been able to cope, even when stressed. Perhaps we need to look at what is going on here that is leading group members to lose sight of the parts of themselves that function adaptively."

In ACOA groups in which members have greater psychopathology, other kinds of structuring and "cooling out" activities on the part of the leaders may also be useful to help lower patient's fears about things getting "out of control." These techniques will be discussed in Chapter 8.

The Problem Is Outside of Me

As noted previously, the ACOA focus provides patients, particularly initially, with a focus outside the self. For many patients, externalization is a comfortable and preferable alternative to the self-blame that they have been riddled with for years. For some, it appears that there is now an understandable "cause" for their problems. Thus, particularly in the early phases of group life, there may be considerable focus on blaming the parents (both the parents of childhood and the parents of the present, who continue to perpetuate the crimes of the past). Along with this, group members may spend time focusing on attempts to change members of their families of origin, and may find it difficult to focus on themselves. When this happens, it may be useful for group leaders to refocus the group with comments such as, "The family members who are not present in this group seem to get considerably more attention than those who are here. My hunch is that the troublesome family members that we are hearing so much about have always gotten more than their fair share of the attention. What would it be like for the family members who *are* here if more of the focus were to be on you."

Another even more focused kind of externalization takes place in some patients who see alcohol *itself* as the externalized bad object. With these patients, the definition of "what's the matter" is even narrower and can also be used as a powerful defense against seeing the bigger picture. For example:

> One of our group members, who had a particularly conflictual relationship with his idealized alcoholic father, developed a nearly paranoid obsession with alcohol — viewing it as a poison to be avoided at all cost. His circumscribed and narrow view of the "toxic object" thus protected him from devaluing the family member who had become addicted.
>
> The view that "alcohol is the enemy" was also evident in another group of ACOAs who met in a clinic room decorated with alcoholism posters. Much group attention was paid to the offensiveness of a particular poster picturing a bottle of hard liquor, with repeated wishes expressed that the leaders might somehow be able to get rid of this noxious stimulus.

Will the Leader Understand? (Therapist Transparency about Her Own Past)

In the early stages of group life, members often express "curiosity" about the group leader and her past* — particularly about

---

*This issue has also been addressed with regard to the concerns of alcoholic group members in Vannicelli (1982).

whether the leader herself is an ACOA. The question relates, in part, to patients' concerns about whether the therapist has had the same kind of unpredictable parenting that they have had — and whether, in turn, the therapist will replicate that erratic parenting in the group, as some members find themselves doing in relationship to their own children. Even the positive, initially good therapist (the idealized leader) may come to be viewed with suspicion. Group members may feel, "You've been good tonight, active, responsive, done things the way we like — but will you stay this way beyond the first few sessions." It is as if members are communicating that they do not want to count on something that will disappear. Their own concerns about inconsistent parenting are thus projected onto the leader, with the particular concern that the leader may be as inept as their own parents (and as they may be with their own children.) For the ACOA who has experienced inconsistency in parenting, the question may periodically resurface regarding how consistent the leader will be — since even good things often turn bad.

Concerns about consistency and predictability of the leader can be addressed, in part, by the general demeanor of the leader with regard to consistency (as discussed in Chapter 6 with regard to limit setting, clear boundaries, etc.). Many leaders may also be tempted to answer questions about their ACOA status directly. However, whether one answers or not, it is essential to take up the underlying concern that is being expressed about the therapist's ability to understand and to help.

A simple "straightforward" response may convince the patient that he cannot get the kind of help that he needs. For example, if the leader says, "I'm not an ACOA," the patient may feel, "How can you possibly understand what I've been through when you have no idea what it is like to live with an alcoholic parent." Even the response, "I too am an ACOA," may be a double-edged sword. While for some patients this may initially seem like the only acceptable answer, for others it may signal that the therapist is "no better off than we are" and "not equipped to care for us."

In all likelihood, the reason that this question is frequently handled as if there is nothing more to it than simple curiosity is that many therapists are persuaded by the success of the many alcohol-related self-help groups available (AA, Al-Anon, and Al-Anon/ACOA groups), where, indeed, all help *is* provided by others with similar problems. Thus, the therapist who would ordinarily explore or interpret similar questions from other patients (e.g., from a mother who wants to know if the therapist has trouble with her adolescents) may neglect to explore requests from ACOA patients regarding the therapist's family of origin. However, it is essential to interpret for the ACOA, as it would be in the parallel instance for the non-ACOA, the concerns underlying these questions about the therapist.

Concerns about Early Problem Drinking

Unlike many alcoholics, who are often the last to be aware of the severity of their problems with alcohol, ACOAs may have a heightened sensitivity regarding potential problematic use of alcohol and other drugs. Often, even when friends and family are unconcerned about the quantity and frequency of the ACOA's substance use, the ACOA, himself, will be worried and anxious about his use of chemical substances. Thus, for example, some ACOAs may find themselves drinking only an occasional beer — but when their quantity exceeds this even slightly (e.g., occasions on which they might have two drinks) or when they find themselves doing this more than once or twice a week, they feel quite concerned about their potential for alcohol abuse. While abstinence is not necessarily the only appropriate solution for these ACOAs, when the situation has come up in our groups, members have often been effective in helping such individuals either to abstain or to set limits on their drinking that they feel more comfortable with. It may also be useful for the leaders to ask why, if the drinking seems to cause such discomfort, the person continues to drink.

Group Defensive Maneuvers

Perseverating around the ACOA Theme

It is common in the early stages of group therapy with ACOAs for family "war stories" to be the primary group theme. Group members establish a sense of cohesiveness by focusing on the one thing known to be held in common — the trials of living with an alcoholic parent. In addition, the group members have picked a relatively safe way of beginning their involvement in the group; the discussion is, indeed, relevant to part of the group task.*

At times, however, a group may persist in focusing on the externalized "bad parent" theme long beyond the first few weeks of the group, or may relapse to this limited form of interaction at times of stress in the group. When this happens, leaders often experience a sense of bewilderment: the group feels stuck and is usually dull, yet it appears to be doing at least part of what it is supposed to be doing. (After all, what could be more legitimate than discussions about how bad Dad's drinking was, his frequent broken promises, etc., in a treatment group for adult children of alcoholics?)

Another common example of defensive ACOA talk is the following. In the middle of an intense, affectively loaded exchange between two group members, another member interrupts to ask, "What does all this have to do with our ACOA issues?" This question is heralded by a chorus of support from other group members. The group leaders should immediately recognize that this protest is a defense against painful feelings that are being stirred up, and that it expresses a wish to return to safer territory. It is, of course, the apparent legitimacy of the parental focus that makes it such a beguiling group defense against exploring deeper issues and achieving greater intimacy.

While it is often difficult to differentiate defensive talk about parents from appropriate discussions of family issues, the two can and must be differentiated. Defensive family focus is characterized by the presence of any of the following: (1) using an ACOA or family-related focus as a distraction (as in the example above); (2) recapping extensive details of past family drinking episodes; (3) detailed reporting of current family problems that engage other group members in extensive "advice giving"; and (4) exclusiveness (i.e., the group seems to be stuck in their families of origin and outside of the group).

---

*This kind of group defensive maneuver has also been discussed in relationship to the treatment of alcoholics (Vannicelli, 1982) and their spouses (Vannicelli, 1987).

In contrast, appropriate discussion of family problems is (1) but one of many areas discussed; (2) characterized by expression and exploration of feelings; and (3) related to here-and-now interactions in the group, as family themes replay themselves in the present.

Other Distraction Activities

There are other times, as well, when discussions occurring within the group, though ostensibly important, can serve as a defense against other more painful material. When the group seems to be eagerly engaged in a topic, yet the leader feels somewhat disengaged and uninterested, this kind of distraction or defensive maneuver may be operating. Even if the leader has no idea what the group is defending against, once she tunes in to the fact that something is missing in the exchange, she might wonder to the group, "What might we be discussing were we not engaged in the topic at hand?"

The following vignette illustrates this kind of distraction activity:

> In one group, following a very intense session in which aspects of a sexualized transference were heatedly discussed, the next session began (and continued for nearly 45 minutes) with members happily chatting about their outside lives — sharing delightful tales of two of the members' new babies, another member's grandchild, and other "updates" from their lives outside the group. When the leader stopped the group halfway through and asked that members examine the territory they had covered during the first half of the group, she was told, "It's been a long time since we've had a chance to check in with one another about our outside lives, and we needed some time to catch up." They went on to talk about how nice it was to get these updates and to be in touch with other aspects of one another. The leader then commented, "Members do seem to enjoy the opportunity to 'catch up' but I wonder whether the length of time spent doing that this week might connect in some way to what was going on in the group during the last session." At that point, group members slowly began to recall the heated discussion from the week before and acknowledged that perhaps it was "too hot" in

the group and that the time spent discussing outside things helped to "cool things down."

Outside-of-group crises may also be used to distract the group from doing the here-and-now processing of perhaps *even more difficult* issues *within* the group. Thus, the patient who presents with one crisis after another from her outside life, while getting the group engaged, also gets it *away from* exploring potentially conflictual within-group issues. It is useful to note that this kind of "distraction activity" may also be used as a defense mechanism in patients' outside lives as a way of managing and distracting themselves from conflict. For example, patients often create chaos in their lives and then complain in therapy about the disarray that they are experiencing. It is often helpful for them to understand that, despite the discomfort of the chaos, this chaos may serve a "distracting" function that keeps them from being in touch with other even more uncomfortable parts of themselves. This distraction can take many forms: taking on too many commitments, creating or precipitating battles at work or with family members, procrastinating to a point where disaster is imminent, etc. But often these self-imposed crises serve the same function — to "distract" against something else that would be even more difficult to look at.

In a similar vein, feelings can also serve as distractions or defenses against other feelings that are even more uncomfortable. For example:

Following a particularly warm session in which a patient became acutely in touch with how much the group therapy (and the leader) meant to her, she came in the next week suspicious about who the leader might be discussing her case with. The leader, noting the marked difference between the tenor of the previous session and the current one (characterized by near-paranoid delusions about the therapist), commented, "As uncomfortable as these untrusting feelings about me might be, I wonder if perhaps they are more comfortable than some others that are even less comfortable." There was palpable relief when the patient smilingly acknowledged that this might be so, and began to talk about her increasing awareness of her tremendous attachment to the group and to the leader. As she put it, "Maybe we got a little too close for comfort last time."

Group Laughter as a Distraction

While laughter can provide a sense of joy and movement to the group, at times it may also serve a defensive function. When the latter appears to be occurring, it may be useful to help group members understand that the laughter may be a way of avoiding painful material. Leaders may say something like the following: "The laughter that is occurring in here right now may be a way of dealing with some of the very difficult things that people have been sharing this evening." Even if the group does not immediately redirect itself to the more difficult material at hand, a comment such as this underscores for the group the seriousness of the issue at hand and the ways in which painful material can be avoided. It also underscores to the individuals whose issues were being processed that they are, indeed, to be taken seriously.

Repetitive, Patterned Interactions

Patterned, repetitive interactions between two or more members may similarly serve a group defensive function. Exchanges of the following variety often serve as a defense against change: "You started it!" "No, you did!" or "I can't stand it when you do X!" "Well I wouldn't do X if you wouldn't do Y." When two or more members in the group get engaged in one of these tightly cyclical and recursive loops, a situation is created in which there is total predictability. Even if the pattern is experienced by all participants as "negative," it protects participating members and the group as a whole against the even more frightening work of moving on and tackling weightier issues. Leaders can often interrupt these recursive loops by asking the participants questions such as the following: "Mr. Smith, did you know what Mr. Jones was likely to say when you said X?" "Mr. Jones, did you know what Mr. Smith was likely to say when you said Y?" Since both participants are likely to answer, "Yes, of course," the therapist would then inquire what use it might serve for them to engage again in this dialogue when the expected outcome is so apparent to both of them (as well as to other members of the group). This kind of distraction activity or defensive maneuver should come to signal to group members that something important is being avoided. It is the leader's task to help the group figure out what that might be and to then move on.

The Assumption of "Sameness"

The assumption of sameness among group members (or between members and leaders) may also be used as a defense against exploring issues in greater depth and against tolerating differences and conflict. Thus, at times of stress in the group, members may attempt to abort further exploration with comments such as, "This is a typical ACOA issue." However, assumptions about "shared understanding" and "sameness" — particularly between the leader (if she is an ACOA) and members — may keep leaders from exploring "the obvious." Thus, a "you know how it is" mentality may develop in the group about "typical ACOAs," leading to tunnel vision and a lack of true exploration. (Some of these issues are exacerbated when the leader is an ACOA or in co-led groups where both leaders are ACOAs.) Because the assumption of sameness may prevent the group from moving from one stage of group life to the next, it is important that leaders challenge this assumption when it emerges. An ACOA label should not be accepted as an adequate summary or explanation of what's going on, but rather, should be understood as the patient's attempt to temporarily close the door on painful issues. Thus, when group members summarize what is going on as, "This is a typical ACOA issue," or "That was a typical ACOA reaction," leaders should ask, "How so?" The leaders should also inquire further about what specifically was going on for the patient in- volved and what additional kinds of feelings or reactions others in the group might have (thus furthering differentiation rather than supporting the defense of "sameness").

While applying a label to behavior can be helpful in provid- ing a mechanism for conceptualization, premature or inexact la- beling may be seen as the kind of defensive soothing that occurs when rationalization is used. Thus labeling, such as,"That's my ACOA behavior," provides a simple surface "explanation" with- out, in fact, really addressing what is going on. As Bader (1988) points out,

. . . labels and catchphrases substitute for real understanding and analysis. A patient will say, "That's my ACA stuff," and invite the therapist to collude under the reassuring pretense that this phrase explains something important, when in actuality it reflects the patient's desire *not* to analyze what s/he is really feeling. (And) . . . short-term relief is purchased at the cost of long-term cure and insight. (p. 98)

Because it is important that labeling not be confused with explaining, when a patient says, "That's my old ACOA behavior," the therapist should ask for more information by inquiring, "How do you mean?" and then following up with, "What do you make of it?" or, "How do you understand your doing this particular thing?" Too often, particularly in groups, the process seems to stop once the label has been applied. It is important that group leaders go beyond the naming to find out more about the real phenomenon.

Refusal to See the Family of Origin (or the Past) as Relevant

Although less common, an interesting defensive maneuver is sometimes used by patients who wish to see all of their problems in terms of their "own biology," rather than connecting their problems, in any way, to their past or to their families of origin.

> In one group a young woman who wished to defend against exploring the psychological issues related to her childhood and the impact of these on her current life, as well as wishing to avoid the intensity of emotional involvement in the group, would focus on biological aspects of her illness whenever things got too heated in the group. Thus, when she became stressed in the group, instead of looking either to the past or to present behavior and interactions to explain what was going on, she would comment, "You doctors want to make this all so complicated. It's clear to me that the reason I have been depressed for the past two weeks is that my medications are not appropriately adjusted. Once my appropriate Lithium levels are reestablished, I will be fine."

Other patients may look to additional mechanisms for "explaining" their current pain, rather than allowing themselves to look to the past, which is even more painful. In such instances, defenses that are already familiar may be invoked, including the use of other diagnoses or clinical labels, such as "My problem is that I'm an obsessive-compulsive personality and that I view everything in a rigid way."

"Smoothing Out" as a Defensive Reaction

Another interesting group defense may be enacted by a member of the group who comes to be known as the "smoother-outer." This individual tries to take the wrinkles out of uncomfortable situations by lowering affect whenever possible. Often this is done by endorsing surface explanations of what is going on in the group, rather than dealing with deeper meanings. For example, the smoother-outer is quick to accept another patient's explanation that he "just forgot to come to group the previous week," following an intense encounter with the leaders the week before. The smoother-outer says, "I get busy and forget important things too." Characteristically, the smoother-outer, in her life outside the group, behaves the same way. Her task is to rescue unstable situations as quickly as possible, to lower tension, to quickly "do for others" in an attempt to help restore a sense of comfort.

The leader's task is to help the group understand the role that the "smoother-outer" plays within the group (both in terms of restoring her own comfort and that of the group), and also to help the particular patient involved to understand how the same behavior serves her in her life outside of the group. It may also be helpful for her to understand that in her haste to "smooth things out" and get rid of every wrinkle as soon as possible, she may be missing out on much of life's richness, both within and outside of the group.

Changing "Time Zones"

In all dynamically oriented (individual or group) therapy, there is continuous movement between present and past, and important work to be accomplished in both arenas. As group members explore present dysfunctional patterns that have repeatedly recurred in their lives, they will gain mastery as they understand how current patterns replicate childhood binds and outmoded solutions. While both past and present are important, each can also be used defensively to take flight from frightening work in the other arena.

The following examples illustrate this kind of defensive activity:

> In one group, in the midst of an intense here-and-now focus in which two members were struggling to express their anger and competitive feelings toward one another, a third member interrupted to say, "I don't really see how Ted and Jane's dislike for one another has anything to do with the work that we're supposed to be doing here. I thought we came here to understand what our parents did to us." This protest can be understood as a defense against fears of emotional overload and a wish to return to safer material.
>
> In another group, when one member began to talk for the first time about her relationship with her father, she struggled through sobs to share painful memories that hinted of sexual abuse. Another member, whose traumatic history shared similar events, interrupted by saying, "You know, Carla, there is just so much you can accomplish by complaining about your parents. We have learned in here that we have to take responsibility for our own lives — regardless of what our folks did or didn't do when we were little."

In both instances, the group has used a seemingly legitimate group focus to defend against painful work. Since both past and present focuses are important and legitimate, it is the leaders' job to know when to help the group move toward one or the other. The group will be most alive and engaging if leaders help it to move toward greater affect — understanding movement away from feelings as a defense. At times, the leaders will simply interpret and explain the defensive maneuvers of the group by saying something like, "It seems as if Carla's memories about these painful times with her dad are hard for the group to stay with. It's a kind of pain that's very familiar to many people in here, and there may be a wish to push it away." At other times, when the leaders feel that the group can stay with the painful feelings, they may try to help the group get back to them. For example, leaders might encourage the group by asking, "What makes it difficult to stay with the feelings?" or, "What thoughts or feelings were others having as Carla talked about her situation with her father?" Clearly, there is a delicate balance between the present and the past; and times when the group defenses will simply be noted, as opposed to other times when the leaders will push for greater exploration.

In addition, at times of severe distress in the group, it may be necessary for the leaders to help the group move *away* from intense affect. This kind of modulation of affect may be necessary with more psychologically impaired populations of ACOAs — particularly in the early phases of group life when patients' fears of becoming "unglued" (as discussed earlier) are at a peak, and the safety of the group has not been adequately established.

Such "modulation techniques" include the following: (1) Periods of heated affect can be neutralized by introducing a more cognitive element. For example, the leader might ask patients about their *thoughts* (as opposed to their feelings); or might ask the group to make observations about what is currently going on in the group or what has transpired during the past few minutes. Similarly, leaders might summarize their own observations about what has transpired in the group. (2) Movement from a present focus to a past focus or from a past focus to a present focus can also be used to diffuse affect in the group. In much the same manner as the leader can move the group *toward* more affect-laden material — choosing past or present focus in such a way as to elevate the feeling tone of the group — the leader can make the same choices in order to cool things down. For example, a patient involved in intense feelings about the past may be moved into a present focus by the leader asking whether she experiences any similar feelings toward current people in her life or toward people in the group (the choice, here, being to move toward the more neutral of the options). Similarly, the patient engaged in a present-focused heated exchange with another group member might be diverted, if it is too intense for the the group or for the particular member to handle, by asking her to think about what, from the past, this reaction might be hooking into.

These modulation techniques involve the leaders' selective use of distracting mechanisms (defensive maneuvers of sorts) to lower the intensity of affect. While these mechanisms are appropriate and useful on occasion (and, thus, skills that leaders should know how to use), it is also important to recognize that, at times, the leaders' feelings that the group process needs to be neutralized may simply resonate with the group's feeling of being out of control. It is thus important for the leaders to be aware of their own countertransference reactions before moving in too quickly to "cool things down."

The next chapter explores countertransference considerations relevant to this issue and relevant to the overall effectiveness of the group leader.

6

Countertransference Considerations

The group leader's countertransference reactions, if understood, can be a tremendous asset in furthering the work of the therapy. If not understood, or recognized, these feelings interfere with successful therapeutic work. This chapter explores, in some detail, the signs of countertransference and the ways in which countertransference reactions are likely to manifest themselves — particularly as reflected in breaks in the therapeutic contract or modification of the basic operating ground rules.

Countertransference Defined

Countertransference, in its broadest terms, may be conceptualized as "the total emotional reaction of the therapist to the patient, with consideration of the (therapist's) entire range of conscious, preconscious, and unconscious attitudes, beliefs, and feelings" . . . (Imhof, Hirsch, & Terenzi, 1983, p. 492). Another definition of countertransference, which may have particular relevance for group therapy with ACOAs because of the intensity of the "family dynamics" that get played out in these groups, comes from the arena of the family therapists. In their work, countertransference is defined as "the family therapist's preconscious perception of the family (that) he or she is treating as if it were his/her family of origin" (Feld, 1982, p. 3). These authors, along with Whitaker, Felder, and Warkentin (1965) and Ferber, Mendelsohn, and Napier (1972), believe that the immediacy of the family therapy elicits responses from the therapist that relate to his or her own family of origin.

As both of these definitions suggest, countertransference is a fact of life for the therapist. When properly understood, it can guide and inform our therapeutic work and can serve as one of the most important tools we have in understanding what is going on for the patient. If not understood, or recognized, these feelings often get in the way of successful therapeutic work.

There are several ways of looking at the different aspects of countertransference and at the roots of the various feelings that our patients stir up in us. As noted earlier, Winnicott's (1949) distinction is one of the most useful. He differentiates between "objective" countertransference reactions and the more "subjective" reactions that the patient creates in the therapist that relate to the therapist's own past and his own personal idiosyncrasies. (We might also think of these subjective reactions as a sort of "transference" that the therapist has to the patient or to the group.) These subjective countertransference feelings, if not adequately attended to, interfere with the therapeutic work.

Objective countertransference reactions, on the other hand, refer to feelings that the patient induces in the therapist that are relevant to the patient's core conflicts and issues. Understanding these induced feelings can pave the way to learning about aspects of the patient's inner life and ways of relating to others that might otherwise be hard to appreciate. As Levine (1988) points out, by creating this differentiation, Winnicott directed therapists' attention to the *interaction* between patient and therapist as a productive arena for exploring important aspects of the patient's dynamics.

Subjective Countertransference

Subjective countertransference, though hopefully minimized both through the therapist's own personal psychotherapy and through supervision, remains an inevitable part of clinical work. As Wynne (1965) points out,

> . . . in his relationship to the constellation of persons seen in family therapy, the therapist cannot so easily bypass partially unresolved countertransference problems.

Either overidentification with a particular family member or a failure to appreciate, understand, and empathize with individuals in a particular family role may create difficulties. (p. 315)

The same can be said of the "family dynamic" and our relationship to it in ACOA therapy groups. For this reason, self-reflection and continuous self-monitoring are necessary. The more we know about our wishes, attitudes, inclinations, and prejudices, the more likely we are to understand what is going on and to be able to use our understanding in a way that is helpful to our patients.

Objective Countertransference

In thinking about objective countertransference, we may view these reactions as encompassing those aspects of the therapist's feelings: (1) that are in reaction to the transference feelings of the patient (i.e., the patient's feelings about significant others in his past as reflected in his feelings about the therapist); and (2) that are set into motion by the therapist's ability to resonate with important feelings that the patient experiences about himself. The latter category includes: (1) feelings of the patient that the therapist directly identifies with, and which by attention to her own emotional response will help her identify with what the patient is feeling (for example the therapist is feeling very sad and understands this to be what the patient is feeling); and (2) feelings that arise in the therapist when the patient projects unwanted aspects of himself onto the therapist, who then takes them in and experiences them as her own. Racker (1968) clarified the distinction between these two differential countertransference responses to the patient's feelings about himself, labeling them *concordant* and *complementary* identifications, respectively.

Concordant identifications are more readily perceived, leading to a direct empathic response (except in those instances in which the therapist herself is defending against knowing the patient's painful feelings). *Complementary identifications* occur through a somewhat more complicated process. To understand this, Racker makes use of the concept of projective identification, a process whereby the patient expels and ejects aspects of himself into the therapist. Although the concept of projective identification has been elaborated in a number of different ways in the literature, Levine's (1988) concise summary of Malin and Grotstein's (1966) conceptualization highlights the importance of investigating the interaction between the patient and therapist. Thus, projective identification is defined (Levine, 1988),

> . . . as a threefold process: (1) there is an unconscious fantasy of projecting a part of oneself into another person . . .; (2) there is a pressure exerted through the interpersonal interaction such that the recipient of the projection experiences pressure to think, feel, and behave congruently with the projection; and (3) after the projection is psychologically metabolized and processed by the recipient, the projected feelings are re-internalized by the projector. (p. 99)

Let us turn now to examine some examples of each of these kinds of objective countertransference. In the first instance, the patient treats the therapist as if she were some other significant actor in his life. Or put another way, he projects onto the therapist feelings that belong to a significant other from the past. An example might be the patient reacting to the therapist angrily, as if she were the bad withholding mother of his past — leading the therapist to feel that she is being viewed unfairly, and that whatever she does will be seen as inadequate. The therapist's reactions to her own feelings may then include thoughts of modifying her clinical approach so as not to be viewed in such a negative light. As Searles (1979) points out,

> . . . when the analyst is being unaccustomedly warmly participative with the patient, we have a clue to the analyst's unconsciously avoiding the negative transference role in which the patient is tending to perceive him (as being, say, a perceivedly remote and unfeeling parent). (p. 579)

In the second category are those feelings that the patient has about himself that influence his interaction with the therapist and, in turn, influence the therapist's feelings. In the case of *concordant* identification, the therapist directly experiences the same feeling as the patient — the patient is sad, the therapist feels the sadness; the patient is enraged at his mother who has abused him terribly, and the therapist experiences that rage, as well. In the case of *complementary* identification (or projective identification), the therapist, as indicated, is induced by the patient to experience many of the unacceptable feelings that the patient experiences about himself. That is, the patient projects out unacceptable aspects of himself in a way such that the therapist identifies with them and experiences them as her own — feeling, and perhaps even acting, as if the projection were accurate. As Grotstein (1981) puts it,

> Powerful feelings are more often than not expressed by giving another person the experience of how one feels. . . . All human beings seem to have the need . . . to be relieved of the burden of unknown, unknowable feelings by being able to express them, literally as well as figuratively into the flesh, so to speak, of the other so that this other person can know how one felt . . . We each are projectors and ultimately wish the other to know the experience (that) we cannot communicate . . . until we have been convinced that the other understands. We cannot be convinced that they understand until we are convinced that they now contain the experience. (pp. 202-203)

This kind of reaction, if understood and appropriately responded to by the therapist, can be extremely useful in helping the patient, not only to feel understood, but also to come to tolerate and accept these feelings within himself. The therapist gets into trouble when she fails to understand that her own feelings and reactions provide important data about the patient. This is especially likely if the therapist herself has unexplored conflicts in similar areas and can no longer keep track of what is her's and what is the patient's.

As an example of projective identification we might consider a therapist's reaction to a patient who insists that he is "getting worse" and that the therapist is "useless" and perhaps even "damaging." The therapist, in reaction to the patient's onslaught, responds with anxiety and comes to feel helpless, inadequate, incompetent, and perhaps even comes to view herself as dangerous or harmful. It is at this point that the therapist has come to understand and to experience how the patient views himself. The patient feels incompetent and inadequate, and he projects these unacceptable aspects of himself onto the therapist by accusing her of "not understanding him," "failing to make him better," and perhaps "making him even worse." The therapist, resonating with these feelings that are being projected onto her, in turn, begins to feel incompetent with this particular patient, to wonder if she knows what she is doing, and to worry that perhaps she *is* making the patient worse. Some of her fears may even be enacted as she, in fact, begins to actually make mistakes, to fluster and to blunder, in ways that are otherwise not characteristic. This validates the patient's projections and completes the interactive loop.

What can also be seen from this brief example is that projective identification, in contrast to simple projection, involves two people and is truly dyadic in nature. As Levine (1988) points out, projective identification is distinguished from projection "in its reliance on the other person's active participation in the defensive operation" (p. 99). Projection need only involve a single person — the projector. It can operate in a vacuum. Unacceptable feelings can be projected out, even onto inanimate objects (for example, magazine pictures). No reciprocal reaction is required. Thus, for example, an angry, hostile patient may see others (including the therapist) as angry and hostile, in the absence of any particular confirming behavior on the part of these others. In contrast, projective identification occurs in an interactional context. There is a dyadic interaction in which the patient puts out unacceptable aspects of himself (the projection), and the therapist receives this (and in someway identifies or resonates with it) and acts or feels accordingly. Two people are involved; and the therapist, by understanding what is going on between herself and the patient has a unique opportunity to understand important aspects of the patient's dynamics.

An example of projective identification which captures something of the subtlety and complexity of the process is provided in Searles' (1979) description of his intense reactions to a particular patient.

> . . . I used often to feel admiration, bordering on awe, for his ability to make nice differentiations in his thoughts, his fantasies, his memories. The subtlety of his thought, and his ability to create beautifully apt metaphors to express his ideas, all seemed quite beyond my reach.
>
> Here again, transference data which emerged subsequently led me to realize, to my great relief, how powerfully motivated he had been to project upon me the feelings of inadequacy which he had felt toward an older brother . . . who had lived, during the patient's childhood, in a longed-for world which felt utterly beyond the younger boy's despairing reach. I now became more aware of the defensive aspects of the patient's functioning during the sessions . . . and was better able

to see . . . his displaying so complex a mental activity . . . (as) designed, more, to shut me out of his world. (p. 580)

Importance of a Continuously Self-Reflective Stance

From all that we have pointed to in the discussions above, it is clear that the therapist who works most effectively with his patients will be one who can maintain a continuously self-reflective stance, examining his own feelings and attitudes in response to the patient. In the interaction between the patient and therapist it is essential to continuously monitor the dynamic process and interaction between the two — what the patient projects out, what belongs to the therapist, and what is the interface or interaction between the two. One's own personal therapy experience is an invaluable aid in this task. As Imhof et al. (1983) suggest,

> While . . . debate (continues) regarding whether or not having personal therapy is a prerequisite to providing therapy, we maintain that only through an examination of one's own emotional development can the therapist most effectively recognize, tolerate, and begin to sort out the infinite range of countertransferential and attitudinal considerations . . . (p. 507)

These authors, discussing the clinical complications involved in working with substance-abusing patients, also point to the tremendous importance of supervision.

> Given the endemic and epidemic nature of substance abuse in society today, it is no longer unlikely that a member of the therapist's family may have a serious problem with drug abuse, including alcoholism. In such instances, there is an even greater need for heightened awareness of countertransferential and attitudinal derivatives emanating from the therapist's personal life. It is imperative to recognize to what extent, if any, a therapist's own personal issues become intertwined with the separate treatment issues of the patient, and in this area clinical supervision can again play a most significant role. (pp. 507-508)

Clearly, when we are talking about work with ACOAs, we are facing identical problems regarding the likelihood of therapist resonation with patient issues and the likelihood of countertransferential complications that need to be carefully monitored and attended to.

Cutting across the various kinds of countertransference, it should be noted that regardless of whether we are talking about objective or subjective countertransference, at times the therapist will initially be more aware of the defense *against* his countertransference feelings than of the countertransference feelings themselves. For example, the therapist may be aware of feeling excessively conciliatory as a defense against his countertransference rage; or the therapist may be aware of feeling overly concerned about "helping and caretaking" in the face of an angry, denigrating patient who is accusing the therapist of being "worthless." In these instances it takes careful self-reflection and self-scrutiny to understand the countertransference feeling and its meaning for the patient.

It should also be noted that the distinctions between subjective and objective countertransference, as well as any of the other countertransference distinctions that we have made, are independent of whether countertransference reactions get in the way or not. Any countertransference reaction that is not understood impedes the work of the therapy — subjective, because it may actually obscure or get in the way of understanding the patient; objective, because valuable information about the patient and his interactions are lost. In this regard, it should also be noted that unexplored positive countertransference feelings — viewing a patient as "sexy as hell" or "a real sweetheart" may be as troublesome as unexplored negative reactions. On the other hand, countertransference that is understood — whether subjective or objective, positive or negative — furthers the work of the therapy by clarifying what is transpiring between the therapist and the patient.

Heightened Countertransference Reactions in ACOA Therapy Groups

It should be clear from the discussion above that when we are talking about countertransference feelings, we are not talking about "good" or "bad" reactions on the part of the therapist.

Rather, we are talking about the therapist's reactions to and resonation with the patient, and the importance of understanding these reactions in order to maximize therapeutic effectiveness. Although the potential for powerful reactions to the patient and resonation with his material exist in individual therapy, as well as in group, this kind of resonation is often particularly intense in group therapy. I like to think of this as similar to the infinitely greater number of possibilities for resonance that occur in a large chamber ensemble than might be likely when a single instrument is playing the same tune. The more parts or voices, the greater the potential for resonance. The potential for this kind of resonance clearly occurs in all therapy — but it is probably heightened in group therapy, and for many therapists is heightened even more in ACOA therapy groups. The latter, I believe, has to do with the fact that, in one way or another, all therapists are "adult-children" wishing to address something that was dysfunctional in their own families of origin. Thus, the powerful family dynamics in ACOA therapy groups are likely to pull for even greater countertransference reactions on the part of group leaders.

Signals of Countertransference

Tip offs to the presence of countertransference can be found by monitoring both the covert and overt responses of the therapist. Covert signs include: (1) unexpected shifts in attitude toward the patient which feel somewhat capricious to the therapist; (2) preoccupation with a given patient or group as expressed through dreams, recurring thoughts, or rehashes in one's head about a session or a portion of a session (i.e., the feeling that one cannot get a particular patient, or group, out of one's mind); and (3) feeling mired down, exhausted, or stuck, or having fantasies about missing a session. Overt signs of countertransference include: (1) stereotyped or fixed responses to the patient, despite variations in the material that the patient brings in or how he presents it; (2) inappropriate affective responses to the patient (i.e., responses that differ from the therapist's usual behavior); and (3) changes in the therapeutic contract — therapist's lateness, sleepiness during the hour, changing the time of appointments or cutting them short, neglecting to return phone calls, and laxness about the patient's failure to respect the therapeutic contract.

As Langs (1975) indicates, the manner in which the basic framework and boundaries of the therapeutic setting are managed (or mismanaged) provides important information about the countertransferential reactions of the therapist. That is, whenever the basic therapeutic contract is broken or the ground rules are modified, by either the patient or the therapist, the specter of countertransference is raised. Obviously, examining these kinds of modifications will be facilitated if the therapist and the patient have a clear idea of what the basic ground rules are. (For this reason these will be addressed in considerably more detail in the exercises that follow.) What is important for the present discussion is that changes or modifications in the way that the therapist operates (or allows his patients to operate) may give clue to important countertransference reactions. This is highlighted by Searles (1979), who states that when the therapist

> . . . finds himself departing from this normative style, in his work with any one patient, (this) provides him with particularly valuable clues to the nature and intensity of this patient's transference responses and attitudes towards him. (p. 578)

Self-Reflection Exercises

Because understanding countertransference requires a self-reflective stance with regard to modifications that we introduce into the therapy (or that we allow the patient to introduce), it is important to have a clear understanding of: (1) what the operating ground rules are, (2) how these ground rules are (or are not) communicated, and (3) how we handle their modification (both the changes that we have intended and those, initiated by the patient, that we have ignored). The exercises that follow are intended to help explore these issues.

To begin this process it may be useful to take a self-conscious look at the expectations that you have for yourself and your clients. It is also helpful to examine: (1) the ways in which these expectations may differ from one population to another (e.g., are they different for ACOAs than for other clients, or for sicker than for healthier clients, or for patients whom you are treating in group rather than in individual therapy?); and (2) when these ground rules get bent or loosened up.

Thinking more specifically about the precise parameters of what we consider to be reasonable and acceptable clinical practice helps us to understand the important turns in the therapy where deviations from the ground rules occur. It is frequently the case that where "slippage" occurs the patient is at an important turning point in expressing one of his major conflicts. An important transference reaction is occurring, and, as indicated by our allowing the slippage to occur, meaningful countertransference, as well. By having a clear set of ground rules, we maximize the opportunity to clearly see, and to productively utilize, the transference and countertransference phenomena as they emerge.

Of all dynamically oriented therapists, group therapists have been traditionally the most explicit about stating their operating ground rules (though, even here, many of the rules are not made explicit). The reason is probably related to the tremendous need, experienced by group therapists, for clear boundaries in an arena in which so much is going on and so many people need to be "tracked." The same principles hold in our individual work with patients, but in our individual work we tend to be less self-conscious about the ground rules — especially as we get further away from our supervisors and further from feeling the need for careful accountability.

On Worksheet 2 you are asked to specify the expectations that you have of your patients as well as the expectations that you have of yourself as a therapist, and, also, to indicate how explicit these expectations are. We know that some expectations are communicated only by subtle aspects of our behavior and are never made explicit (i.e., covert expectations). Other expectations are explicitly stated in the first or second session, and still others are explicitly stated but not until later in the therapeutic work when it appears necessary in order to get past a "hurdle" that has developed. It should be noted that having a clear set of expectations for yourself and your patients is important even if some of these expectations are covert.

Therapists often have different sets of expectations (both for their patient and for themselves) for different populations that they work with. If your expectations for subgroups of patients are differentiated in this way, make additional copies of Worksheet 2 and fill them out separately for each population.

WORKSHEET 2   Therapist and Patient Expectations and Explicitness

Population _____
(specify which population this set of ground rules applies to)

Expectations of patient	Explicit as part of initial contract	Explicit as it comes up	Not explicit
1._____	_____	_____	_____
2._____	_____	_____	_____
3._____	_____	_____	_____
4._____	_____	_____	_____
5._____	_____	_____	_____
6._____	_____	_____	_____
7._____	_____	_____	_____
8._____	_____	_____	_____

Expectations of therapist (of yourself)

1._____	_____	_____	_____
2._____	_____	_____	_____
3._____	_____	_____	_____
4._____	_____	_____	_____
5._____	_____	_____	_____
6._____	_____	_____	_____
7._____	_____	_____	_____
8._____	_____	_____	_____

Having completed the first exercise (Worksheet 2) now take a look at Table 2, Ground Rules to Consider, and see if there are any ground rules on this list that you inadvertently omitted on Worksheet 2 — that is, issues that you generally *do* consider, even if not made explicit with each patient. Go back and add any that you missed to Worksheet 2.

TABLE 2 Ground Rules to Consider

EXPECTATIONS FOR PATIENT

1. *Fees*
    a. Amount of fee
    b. Fee increases (frequency and amount)
    c. Fee reductions (basis for decision and criteria for reevaluation)
    d. Payment schedule (weekly, monthly)
    e. Payment format (mailed in response to bill, paid at beginning of session, paid at end of session)
    f. Policy regarding owing money
    g. Amount of advance notice to avoid paying for canceled sessions
    h. How insurance forms will be handled

2. *Frequency of sessions*
    a. Number of sessions per week
    b. Scheduling additional time when needed
    c. Policy regarding sessions that fall on Holidays.

3. *Between-session contacts*
    a. Scheduling extra time
    b. Availability for telephone contact
        (1) Length of calls and frequency that will be permitted
        (2) Whether calls will be charged or not
        (3) Hours that are permissible (anytime day or night? weekends?)
    c. Outside contact (and socializing) among group members

4. *Length of sessions*
    a. Usual length
    b. Session length if patient comes late

5. *Regularity of attendance and promptness* (especially important for group)

6. *Initial evaluation* (specifying number of sessions to decide if therapist and the patient will work together)

7. *Length of treatment*

8. *Expectations regarding what and how patient will share*
    a. How silences will be dealt with
    b. Whether patient is told he is there to talk about whatever comes to mind and that he will provide the agenda

(cont.)

TABLE 2   (cont.)

9. *Talking about, rather than acting on, feelings*
   a. Physical contact
   b. Threatening or destructively abusive verbal behavior

10. *Confidentiality* (especially important for group)

11. *Planning termination* (especially important for group)

EXPECTATIONS FOR THERAPIST

1. *Reliability* (keeping appointments)

2. *Promptness* (on time for appointments)
   a. How therapist will handle sessions that he comes late for (will time be made up?)

4. *Therapist's self-disclosure*
   a. Topics that are acceptable
   b. Topics that are not acceptable
   c. Whether this will be addressed at the outset or will come up topic by topic

5. *Physical contact*
   a. Handshakes
   b. Hand on shoulder
   c. Other

6. *Giving advice*
   a. About what topics
   b. When this is considered appropriate

7. *Rescheduling appointments*
   a. Based on patient's needs
   b. Based on therapist's needs

8. *Returning phone messages* (how soon?)

9. *Confidentiality* (with whom the therapist will discuss the case and release-of-information forms)

10. *Keeping awake and alert during sessions*

Finally, on Worksheet 2a, list any additional ground rules that you have *not* been attending to but which, after reviewing Table 2, you now feel may be important in your work with patients. Again make additional copies, as needed, for separate populations.

WORKSHEET 2a Additional Therapist and Patient Expectations that Should Be Part of the Working Contract

Population _____
(specify which population this set of ground rules applies to)

Expectations of patient	Explicit as part of initial contract	Explicit as it comes up	Not explicit
1._____	_____	_____	_____
2._____	_____	_____	_____
3._____	_____	_____	_____
4._____	_____	_____	_____
5._____	_____	_____	_____
6._____	_____	_____	_____
7._____	_____	_____	_____
8._____	_____	_____	_____

Expectations of therapist (of yourself)

1._____	_____	_____	_____
2._____	_____	_____	_____
3._____	_____	_____	_____
4._____	_____	_____	_____
5._____	_____	_____	_____
6._____	_____	_____	_____
7._____	_____	_____	_____
8._____	_____	_____	_____

Having completed these exercises, you will no doubt notice some interesting things about the operating ground rules that guide your therapeutic practice. Some of the questions that you will want to consider are the following:

1. What kinds of expectations are you inclined to make explicit and which are more likely not to be made explicit?
2. What differences are there, if any, from one population or subgroup that you work with to the next? How clear are you about your criteria for differentiating your ground rules by population? Are the differences really justifiable or do they reflect countertransference-based differences in your expectations of various subgroups?
3. Do you have different expectations for patients whom you consider to be sicker, or for patients who have more money (or conversely, those whom you see as more disadvantaged)? Are these differences justified?
4. Are there areas in which explicit guidelines have been lacking where you now feel they should be included? Do you see any pattern in your omissions?

Ground rules are intended as guidelines for the patient and the therapist. At one time or another they may be loosened up, modified, or changed. Worksheet 3 examines modifications or infractions of the contract and the degree to which you, as a therapist, were intentionally (consciously) involved in making a decision about the change in procedure.

On Worksheet 3 list each expectation (from Worksheets 2 and 2a) in which infractions or modifications occurred. Then indicate whether each modification was consciously considered and an active decision made (Columns 1 and 2) or if, in fact, the infraction occurred without any decision one way or another on your part — that is, a change was introduced by the patient and more or less inadvertently ignored by you (Column 3). It should be noted that Columns 1 and 2 both involve active decision-making on your part. They differ, however, in that column 1 reflects changes that the therapist felt were indicated and actively initiated, or which he endorsed after the patient initiated them; and Column 2 reflects changes that the patient initiated which the therapist *decided* could be ignored.

WORKSHEET 3   Modifications or Infractions of Contract and Degree of Therapist Intentionality

Population _____
(specify which population this set of ground rules applies to)

	Degree of therapist intentionality		
Patient infractions	Therapist decided a change was indicated (1)	Therapist decided to ignore (2)	Therapist inadvertently ignored (3)
1._____	_____	_____	_____
2._____	_____	_____	_____
3._____	_____	_____	_____
4._____	_____	_____	_____
5._____	_____	_____	_____
6._____	_____	_____	_____
7._____	_____	_____	_____
8._____	_____	_____	_____

Therapist infractions

1._____	_____	_____	_____
2._____	_____	_____	_____
3._____	_____	_____	_____
4._____	_____	_____	_____
5._____	_____	_____	_____
6._____	_____	_____	_____
7._____	_____	_____	_____
8._____	_____	_____	_____

In the three columns following each infraction, put a check mark for each instance that you recall. Thus, for example, if one of the infractions that frequently occurred was exceeding the limits regarding "between-session phone contacts," you might have one or two checks in Column 1 (indicating that you felt that the change was indicated) and perhaps ten or twelve instances that belong in Column 3.

Again, if you have different ground rules for different populations, and if the infractions also differ by population, make additional copies of Worksheet 3 and fill them out separately for each population.

Now, for each item on Worksheet 3 in which conscious decisions were involved, use Worksheet 3a to briefly list the factors that you considered. Again, if warranted, do separately by population.

WORKSHEET 3a Modifications or Infractions of Contract: Factors Considered

Population _____
(specify which population these infractions occur with)

Patient infractions   Factors considered

1._____   _____

2._____   _____

3._____   _____

4._____   _____

5._____   _____

6._____   _____

7._____   _____

8._____   _____

Therapist infractions

1._____   _____

2._____   _____

3._____   _____

4._____   _____

5._____   _____

6._____   _____

7._____   _____

8._____   _____

Now go back and review both Worksheet 3 and 3a. Are there any common themes or patterns? If you have described more than one population, take a close look at the ground rules that you specified, the infractions, and your justifications. Are there differences by population? What did you learn about *yourself* from these exercises? If you do have more than one set of ground rules, to what extent are they based on different attitudes, feelings, and expectations about various groups of patients? These probably reflect years of experience and ways of operating — but are they justified?

These are the kinds of questions it is important to consider in order to understand the baseline expectations with which we begin therapy relationships — and which substantially influence the psychotherapy work that ensues. It is also important to be clear about the ground rules, so that we know when slippage has occurred — and hopefully, with reflection, will also have some idea *why*.

The next worksheet will help you examine the consequences of instances in which you loosened the ground rules. Clearly, not all modifications of our operating ground rules are bad. Flexibility is essential. In fact, conscious modification of a ground rule after careful thought (perhaps following discussion with a respected colleague) can be very helpful. The other kind of slippage usually reflects some important piece of work that is getting *played out* (instead of talked about) between you and the patient. Frequently, understanding unintended slippage will help focus the key aspects of the treatment.

On Worksheet 4, indicate for each occasion in which you loosened the rules (either about your behavior or the patient's), whether or not the modification was useful in the therapeutic work, and why. Again, make additional copies of the worksheet, as needed for separate populations.

WORKSHEET 4   Utility of Loosening the Rules (Infractions)

Population _____
        (specify which population these infractions occur with)

Patient infractions	Useful yes	no	Why useful or not
1._____	☐	☐	_____
2._____	☐	☐	_____
3._____	☐	☐	_____
4._____	☐	☐	_____
5._____	☐	☐	_____
6._____	☐	☐	_____
7._____	☐	☐	_____
8._____	☐	☐	_____

Therapist infractions

	Useful yes	no	
1._____	☐	☐	_____
2._____	☐	☐	_____
3._____	☐	☐	_____
4._____	☐	☐	_____
5._____	☐	☐	_____
6._____	☐	☐	_____
7._____	☐	☐	_____
8._____	☐	☐	_____

Now go back and examine your worksheets to see what they tell you about: (1) differences in utility of certain kinds of modifications as opposed to others; (2) differences in utility when the modification was *planned* in advance as opposed to just happening (you may want to refer back to Worksheet 3 to help you examine this); (3) differences between modifications that you made for various subgroups; and (4) differences when it was a modification in your behavior as opposed to a modification in the patient's behavior.

Therapists' Experiences While Completing These Exercises

As you have been completing these exercises, you have no doubt been asking yourself some important questions about your own work, and may also have wondered about other peoples' experiences in filling out these worksheets. One very senior therapist that I worked with said, after completing the first exercise, "I'm really surprised to see how little I've made explicit — even to myself!" Another responded, "What shocks me is that the only thing I really make *explicit* to the patient is the fee. Surely that cannot be the most important thing that we both understand about our working relationship!" (Many of the therapists that I have worked with have found that issues around fee setting tend to be the most explicit — but that even here, there is a lot of vagueness around (1) when the bill will be paid, (2) what happens when it is late, (3) how much of a debt can be accrued before action is taken, etc.)

Another therapist's reaction to these exercises was to ponder, "I feel I do have rules — but as I'm doing this, I also realize that they vary so much from one client to the next, for reasons that I'm not even aware of, that I'm not sure I really stay on top of any of it." Yet another therapist said, "You know, I do have rules about such things as 24-hour notice for cancellations, make-up appointments, etc., and I think I tell these to most of my patients. But then, I am not always sure who I have explicitly told and who I have not. Thus, when a problem comes up, I often feel a little embarrassed when the patient seems confused about the rules, and wonder whether, in fact, I really did make it clear."

Confusion about the rules is common among therapists and,

as I have pointed out, contributes to even greater confusion and frustration later on when the patient appears to be breaking one (or is he?). Since I have never met a therapist who did not know the fee that he was charging each patient (somehow we all have a way of writing this down in a place that we can keep track of), it is puzzling to me how many other areas therapists often feel they do make explicit but have not actually written down — a situation that often leads to later confusion. Even if you do not take notes after each session, it is a good idea, when first beginning with a patient, to have a check list of areas that you want to be sure you cover and about which you make a notation to yourself. Surely, you would not think of *not* writing down the fee that you have agreed to, and I have never known a therapist who did not have his patient's name (generally spelled correctly), address, and phone number (usually work and home), as well as insurance information. In other words, there are many things that do get written down, and whatever system you use for noting these can (and should) also make provisions for noting aspects of the working agreement that you have made explicit with the patient. This information — perhaps as a face sheet — should be placed at the front of each patient's chart so that any time an infraction seems to occur you can easily check your records to see whether, in fact, it really is an infraction. (See Appendix D for a sample clinical face sheet.)

On occasion, I have found myself uncertain about how explicit I have been — for example after six months without a cancellation, a patient calls in a half-hour before his appointment to say that he is sick and will not be able to attend. I immediately check my notes on that patient to be *sure* that I have made explicit my 24-hour cancellation policy. If I do not find specific notation in my records, I think that there is at least a chance that I have not made the policy explicit to the patient. I would handle this by asking the patient at his next visit whether, in fact, I had clarified this aspect of my billing policy, indicating that I was not sure myself that I had. If the patient says that I did not, I would let him know that in this instance I would not charge for the missed session; but that since my policy is to charge unless I have 24-hour notice, in the future that would be how we would operate. On the other hand, if I found that I *had* noted it in my records and the patient said he knew nothing about it, I would either charge for the missed session, reclarifying our contract, or I might decide that since the patient was unclear about our agreement I would give him the benefit of the doubt (only *his* doubt at this point). I would then process with him what he thought it might mean that he had forgotten about our having discussed it, and raise the possibility that he might have had some feelings right from the beginning about this particular policy.

With group patients, clarifying the ground rules is frequently handled (as discussed in Chapter 3) by a verbal itemization in the pregroup interview, accompanied by a set of written guidelines for the patient to keep (see Appendix C). Written guidelines such as this (possibly adaptable to work with individual clients as well) do not, of course, prevent infractions of the ground rules, but do make it more clear when an infraction has occurred.

Clearly, even with an area as simple and clear-cut as the cancellation policy, it is easy to see the kind of difficulty that the therapist can get into if he is not sure himself about whether or not things have been made explicit. It is our own fogginess about the rules that causes the greatest difficulties in our work with patients. If we are clear about our own expectations and behave consistently with regard to the ground rules, patient slips can be handled therapeutically and in a manner that maximizes the opportunity to understand the deviations that do occur. When we are foggy about the rules, it is much more difficult to productively examine the slippage that occurs.

Importance of Clear Boundaries and Consistency of Ground Rules in the Treatment of ACOAs

It is a sine qua non of all good psychotherapy that the therapeutic context provide a stable, predictable environment in which the patient can feel safe and adequately "contained." In particular, when working with patients who have grown up in dysfunctional families that are characterized by unpredictability and unreliability, it is important for the therapist to be sure that "his house" (as represented in the therapy hour) is in order. As Wood (1987) underscores in discussing her work with ACOAs, "It goes without saying that if the therapist does prove to be erratic or unreliable in some important way, frequently canceling or rescheduling appointments for example . . . there will be an immediate and deleterious effect on the work" (p. 113).

It is for this reason that so much attention has been directed in these pages to having a clearly articulated set of operating ground rules to guide the therapist's work. It is important that the therapist behave in a consistent and predictable way with regard to the ground rules once they have been established, and, if a modification seems to be needed, that he take adequate stock of the therapeutic implications of making a change.

Changing the Ground Rules

Although it is important to have a clear set of ground rules so that both you and the patient know what to expect, there will be times when it may be appropriate to modify these. For example, when a patient is in crisis, it *may* be indicated to see him more often. However, even an "obvious" change such as this should be thought about carefully. As Langs (1975) cautions in his detailed discussion about the importance of maintaining a consistent clinical framework,

> . . . deviations . . . should be limited to . . . relatively rare clinical situations . . . (after) the therapist's countertransference has been carefully subjected to self-analysis. . . . Before deviating, a full consideration of all other disturbing factors should be made, since problems within the therapist and with his technique are often more important to the stalemate than the psychopathology of the patient.
>
> In . . . those circumstances where the therapist formulates the need for a deviation . . . he should counterbalance his assessment of the indications for the deviation with a full anticipation of the possible negative consequences. (pp. 118-119)

It is important that the therapist be able to modify the ground rules, when indicated, and also that he think creatively about possible modifications. Take, for example, a patient who is seemingly getting more and more distraught, but who is talking less and less in the therapy sessions. Such was the case with an ACOA patient whose therapist I saw in consultation some years ago.

The therapist was coming to almost dread the sessions because the patient (who functioned on the outside as a chemist in a very demanding research laboratory) regressed during the therapy hours, stammering out initial monologues at the beginning of each session such as the following: "I . . . can't . . . talk . . . anymore . . .", and then produced relatively little additional material until the last 10 or 15 minutes of the hour. The therapist, sensing her patient's increasing distress (the patient was also calling with similar kinds of messages several times a week at late hours) offered to give him a second appointment each week. Since the patient had limited financial resources, the therapist also lowered the fee.

Clearly, the modifications that were introduced into the therapy were directly related to the therapist's perception of the patient's pain and distress (and possibly to the therapist's own countertransference reactions to this as well). As a result, the therapist was now facing *two* hours a week during which the patient's behavior repeated the same frustrating pattern.

Thinking creatively, one could imagine other solutions that might have served the therapy better. What if, for example, the therapist had responded to her patient's pain, to the fact that he needed more treatment but could not afford to pay for any more, and combined this with an acknowledgment that he often "used" only half of the session that he was currently paying for? Would she have accomplished as much (or more) by offering the patient two half-hour sessions per week at the same fee — thus maintaining the cost to the patient and eliminating the need for a reduction in her fee? She might have suggested to the patient, "You seem to be in considerable distress these days, and in some way your suggestion that we meet more often seems to make sense. On the other hand, I've noticed that it is frequently difficult for you to use the full hour that we do spend together. I wonder whether it might work out better if we were to meet for two briefer sessions per week instead." If the therapist felt that part of the problem was that the patient needed time to "settle" before beginning to talk, she might even suggest that the patient come to her office 15 to 20 minutes prior to the session and sit in the waiting room so that he could get comfortable before the session began.

Alternatively, the therapist might have offered a half-hour individual session per week along with a weekly ACOA therapy group — again addressing her patient's need for more treatment while simultaneously attending to his financial limitations and to his inability to productively use the full hour of the weekly individual session. (The patient would also have gotten the added bonus of being able to work with other ACOAs in a group.) Thinking creatively about modifying the ground rules means that the therapist must consider the patient's needs, her own needs, and what a modification would mean to *both of them*.

Seeking Consultation or Supervision When You Want to Bend a Rule

When you are considering doing something different with your group, or with an individual member of the group, which reflects a deviation from your general operating ground rules, consultation or supervision should be seriously considered. But what kind of supervision or assistance should you seek out? Therapists are sometimes inclined to ask for "consultation" from somebody who they think is likely to support what they want to do — a colleague who they know is "flexible" in the particular area in which they are considering making a change. It is probably a good idea, instead, to pick a colleague or supervisor who you suspect is likely to be a little bit more conservative than you are — someone who may challenge you to think more about what you are doing, rather than simply giving you a green light. In this regard, I am reminded of the story of the sinner who had catalogued all of the confessionals in town, and knew which priests were light on which sins. When he felt he needed to confess, he would pick a church accordingly. While he thus accomplished one of his goals (expiation), the real purpose of seeking out a wise superior was lost.

Noticing Patient-Initiated Modifications

Even relatively subtle modifications in patients' behavior in the group should be attended to. Given the basic premise that the work of the therapy group takes place in the verbal mode and that patients are encouraged to talk, rather than act, *actions* take on special meaning (for example, when a group member suddenly brings her knitting to a therapy session, or dinner in a paper sack, or pulls out a pad and pencil during a session). Under such circumstances a fancy interpretation on the part of the therapist is not usually required. Generally it is adequate to simply observe with something like the following, "I notice that you brought your knitting tonight, Mary, any thoughts about it?" The therapist might also ask what reactions or feelings were stirred up in others when Mary pulled out her knitting. Or, the therapist might ask the patient who decides to "dine" during the group, how bringing her supper to this particular session might relate to what has been going on in the group over the past few weeks (or during the last meeting). If the patient responds, "I don't think it really means anything; I just didn't get a chance to eat before coming tonight," the leader should keep in mind, even if the explanation seems plausible, that the patient's behavior is *unusual* (after all, most adults can wait an hour and a half to eat.) The leader might inquire further by asking other questions such as, "Did you have any thoughts about how the group, or the leader, might respond to your dining in the group tonight?" or, "It sounds like you were concerned that in the various meetings you attended today it would not have been appropriate for you to pull out a sandwich. Did you have any similar thoughts about how it would be perceived in here?" If the patient says, "No, it didn't occur to me," the therapist might pursue further by asking, "Any ideas about why you hadn't thought about that — especially since it is pretty unusual behavior in here?"

No matter what the change in behavior or slippage with regard to the ground rules, the patient has either had thoughts and feelings about it in advance of doing it (and these are obviously important to explore) or he has not (in which case it is interesting to explore why he has not). As group leaders, we are "explorers" on a journey. Nothing that we see along the road is uninteresting — and our interest will be sparked, in particular, by anything that is *unusual*.

It is often especially difficult for therapists to explore those changes in patient behavior that serve the therapist's interests particularly well. (The countertransference implications of this are usually quite easy to see.) For example:

A young male patient toward the middle of his third year of treatment suddenly announced that he thought that I should give him a fee increase. (At that point he was paying about 20% below my usual fee due to financial constraints at the time he presented for treatment.) He volunteered that there had been a couple of salary increases at his part-time job, and that it would thus be "more than fair" for him to now pay the full fee that I deserved.

I was all too happy to have the fee increase, and thought that it was likely that I did "deserve it," especially if what he was describing about his change in salary was accurate. However, I decided that there might be some clinical payoff in exploring the matter further, since his behavior was sufficiently out of character (money was a constant concern as school tuitions were increasing and his alcoholic mother had become increasingly erratic in providing financial assistance). Thus, I responded, "The fee increase certainly does seem like a reasonable possibility, but I'd like to hear more about your thoughts and feelings about it." There followed further "justification" of the increase, which he told me he had decided "seemed only fair" as he was driving home from the previous week's session. At that point I recalled an unusual occurrence that had happened just prior to that meeting. I was standing on the porch outside our clinic and called out a greeting to an attractive young male trainee whom I had been trying to persuade to lead a group in our clinic. I yelled out something like, "Hi Joe, let me know as soon as you can whether you are interested in that opening." My patient walked up just about then and, as we proceeded up the stairs into my office, he made a brief comment about "how nice it was to see me outside of the office and in a different context." During the session I inquired about his thoughts and feelings about seeing me in this different way. He was able to produce very little other than his "pleasure in being able to see me in a fuller context." It should be noted that this patient's feelings and fantasies were always just beneath the surface, but difficult to raise beyond that. (For example, it was not unlike him to suddenly interrupt himself mid-sentence to comment on "how nice my long beads were.") I asked him to share what it was that had been different, what precisely he had noticed on the porch, and all he could come up with was that he had seen me talking to another man who he "figured was another patient."

Remembering this transaction from the previous week, I asked, "Since the changes in your financial situation are not new, but the idea of paying me more is, might this relate in some way to what happened in our last session?" The patient then blushed and said, "Oh no, I don't see how it possibly could." I responded, "Perhaps not, but what do you remember about our last session?" The patient responded, "Nothing in particular — except that it was nice to see *you on the porch that way." Exploring further, the patient then recalled hearing me say to "some other young man" that "there might be an opening coming up soon," adding, "since your time is valuable I'm sure you'd prefer to see someone who would pay the full fee."*

As can be seen, the offer to pay more was only minimally related to "fairness" and finances, but related substantially to other feelings that had been stirred up in the patient (e.g., competitive feelings with another attractive young male whom I might see as "more desirable to work with" and feelings that I might reject or abandon him as his alcoholic mother had done). Had I simply reached closure immediately on his change in behavior (the offer of a fee increase), I might never have understood the many other issues associated with his unusual behavior.

The importance of examining a proposed modification in the fee is again illustrated in the following case vignette.

Another ACOA patient spontaneously suggested, after four months in therapy at half-fee, that he now wished to "pay double" for his therapy sessions. This was coupled with the statement to his therapist that "this would mean, of course, that I would only be able to see you twice a month, no matter what."

This patient was using negotiations around the fee as a way of titrating his dependence on the therapist. (It is of some interest that the suggestion also came at the time that the psychiatrist he met with monthly for medication was leaving for maternity leave — stirring up old feelings about his alcoholic mother's "frequent disappearing acts"). He was thus simultaneously giving his individual therapist a message of her importance to him (she was worth double) while at the same time placing a self-imposed limit on the extent to which he would be able to become dependent on her.

When Patients' Slip-Ups Parallel Similar Slip-Ups by the Therapist

Therapists often find it particularly difficult to bring up boundary infractions in the group which parallel infractions that they, themselves, have made. For example, it is common to hear, "I walked into the group three minutes late, and two or three patients trickled in after I did. I thought I should have dealt with their lateness — but how could I, after being late myself?" Clearly, this is an understandable sentiment on the part of the therapist. It feels uncomfortable to call someone else on a faux pas that we ourselves have committed. On the other hand, therapists are human. We occasionally make mistakes and emergencies come up. We accidentally overschedule. Regardless of whether or not our slipups are avoidable (if avoidable — raising the possibility of a countertransference reaction), it is clearly a mistake to "atone" for our mistakes by overlooking similar mistakes in our patients. The patient's "mistake" or looseness about the rules is either unrelated to our own mistake (and hence relates to only what is going on inside of him), or it *is* directly related to our behavior. In either case, it is important.

If, for example, patient lateness follows a session (or sessions) in which the group leader has been late, the group leader might raise this by saying, "I notice that several people have arrived late tonight (or over the past few weeks). I wonder how this might connect to my own lateness in recent weeks?" Alternatively, the therapist might simply note the lateness and ask what group members make of it. If group members respond with a litany of "legitimate" excuses, she might validate the reality that they present and wonder, in addition, how their being late (or at least their feelings about it) might relate to her own lateness at the last session (or during the past few weeks.) Similarly, a therapist who occasionally makes billing errors (adding up the totals wrong, for example) may feel uncomfortable raising a patient's miscalculation on his payment check. But obviously, the same logic holds. Either the patient's behavior is directly linked to his perception of the therapist's carelessness, and his feelings about it (in which case there is much to explore), or it is independent of the therapist's mistake (in which case there are equally plausible and useful paths to explore).

Handling Therapist Mistakes

It is obviously important that the therapist keep his mistakes to a minimum, and staying on top of countertransference reactions will carry him a long way toward achieving this goal. However, it is equally important, when mistakes do occur, that the therapist is able to be sensitive to his patient's reactions about the mistakes and is able to make the most of them therapeutically. Often small mistakes take on tremendous meaning for our patients.

> An extremely strong reaction occurred in one group when its leader accidentally ran the group 10 minutes overtime one evening. Given the context of great punctuality of this particular group and the five-year history of very clear time boundaries around the group, this deviation was quite noticeable. One member, wishing to protect the leader from perceived "fallibility," wondered if perhaps his watch had "lost time." Another speculated that the leader had done it on purpose in order to stimulate discussion (an explanation which this patient found preferable to the possibility that the leader had actually made a mistake). Other members tried to excuse the leader as "only human" — but upon further exploration were experiencing considerable discomfort about his "fallibility," which they associated with the unpredictability of their alcoholic parents.

As Winnicott (1955/1975) reminds us, "Failures there must be" (p. 298). However, the key to using these therapeutically is to understand that the therapist's present failure is "being used and must be treated as a *past* failure, one that the patient can perceive and encompass, and be angry about now." Winnicott explains the patient's intense anger over seemingly small therapist errors as a way of enabling the patient to be angry about past parental failures. The work of the therapist is, thus, to understand what was needed by the patient (and not forthcoming) at the time the original failure occurred.

Procedures for Dealing with Countertransference (What Do You Do about it?)

Having defined countertransference and having underscored the likelihood of its frequent and intense occurrence in ACOA therapy groups, the well-warned reader might now be wondering what he is supposed to *do* when the inevitable happens. I'd like to discuss this with reference, in particular, to projective identification. There are two important steps in dealing with projective identification. First, the therapist needs to understand what the patient is projecting onto him. By understanding it, he neutralizes and detoxifies the projection, therefore "containing" the unacceptable feelings. Second, the therapist makes an interpretation or com- ment. The first step is the most important. As Searles (1979) points out,

> . . . it is the therapist's own dawning recognition of his "countertrans- ference" — his own contribution to these stalemating processes — that provides the best handle for his effecting a change in the therapeutic relationship . . . (p. 81)

Until complete intellectual and emotional understanding is achieved, the therapist's words will be ineffective, as they will be contradicted by messages that he gives out through other channels. For example, if the therapist understands intellectually what is going on but has not fully metabolized this understanding emo- tionally, he will not be able to neutralize or detoxify the patient's material. When he then makes a statement to the patient, no matter how reasonable the comment may be, he is likely to "leak" through body language or tone of voice the unacceptable affect that has been projected onto him. Thus, the therapist conveys that he is still in the countertransference bind.

A clinical example will help illustrate what I am referring to.

> Many years ago, when I separated from my husband, I removed my wedding band. A few months later, the couples group that I was co-leading seemingly "out of the blue" suggested that we go around the room and find out how many years of collective marital experi- ence we had among us — "including the leaders." As the discussion proceeded, more and more of the group's energy became focused on me. During this time, I was having fleeting thoughts about whether I should be leading a couples group at this point in my life, feeling somewhat "decredentialled" by my own pending divorce. I found myself fantasizing about being on the other side of the door and fleeing after the session, never to return. Alongside of this, my words were quite appropriate (corroborated by my co-therapist, who was mystified himself as to why so much of the questioning seemed to remain focused on me). What was transpiring in the group was that a part of me (the thinking part) had a handle on what was going on and continued to perform "appropriately." Yet,

emotionally, I was very much caught in the feelings of failure, incompetence, and inadequacy that the group members were projecting onto me — and I found myself resonating with these feelings. Through body language and other nonverbal means (messages which contradicted my actual verbal input), I was signaling to the group my countertransference resonation with their issue.

Similar situations often arise when group leaders are given reasonable input from a supervisor, which they are unable to emotionally metabolize. (Sometimes they don't even fully believe the input intellectually, let alone emotionally, but being good trainees, they go back to their groups and say the *words* that the supervisor has suggested.) Inevitably, under these circumstances, the countertransference bind continues. It is often sorted out only later, when the group leader's sense of inadequacy and frustration is then projected onto the supervisor in the next supervisory session. The supervisor then is in a position to sort out what is going on between him and the supervisee and to understand it as a replication of the bind that is occurring between the supervisee and members of the group. We can see from this that in the parallel process that occurs during supervision, another projective-identification dyad is reproduced that closely mirrors the interaction between the group leader and the group members.

I have indicated that the therapist must begin to unravel the countertransference issue by *understanding* the projective identification. But how does he go about this? In my own work, I have found the following three steps helpful. First, I identify that I am in a countertransference bind. There are signals for each of us that indicate that we are "caught up" in something. These include the following: boredom; intense feelings while leading the group (extreme anger, overwhelming sadness, humiliation, etc.); thoughts or feelings about wanting to discontinue leading the group, or to take a vacation from it; anxiety during or prior to the group; feelings of incompetence; preoccupation with the group through dreams or frequent thoughts about it.

The second step, after having identified that I am in a countertransference bind, is to decide to actively *do* something to extricate myself from it. This might include calling a colleague to discuss the clinical situation, contacting a supervisor, or returning to some old familiar text that has been helpful in the past.

The third step is to get a cognitive and emotional handle on what is going on, using the inputs from the second step and working with the material until I fully understand what it is that I am feeling and how this connects to the patient's issues. The calmed understanding that results is then somewhat "miraculously" transmitted to the group. I still marvel at the "magic" of this — yet I think most therapists are aware that communications "leak" to our patients through many channels, in addition to the direct, deliberate verbal communications that we intend to transmit (Alpert, 1970; Blanck & Rosenthal, 1984; Blanck, Rosenthal & Vannicelli, 1986; Ekman, Friesen, O'Sullivan & Scherer, 1980; Snyder, 1946).

In my own experience, I find that once I have identified that I am in a countertransference bind (Step 1), if I pick up an old favorite among my "bibles," Kohut's (1971) *Analysis of the Self,* and "randomly" read through the index and selected portions (Step 2), I inevitably come up with a preliminary explanation of what has been going on between me and the patient. After mulling this over and mastering it cognitively (Step 3), I go into the next group session feeling prepared emotionally, and usually with some brief words that I may be able to use to help clarify what has been going on in the group. Often, once I am clear about what is going on, I find that I do not need to *say* anything. From the time I walk in, I am aware that the countertransference tensions that I had previously been experiencing are substantially mitigated. The group member with whom I was experiencing the tension seems no longer to be caught in it, and often, much to my surprise, that member or another comes up with the exact explanation that I had worked out.

Similarly, group leaders often tell me, following a discussion in supervision about some heated group dynamics (usually involving countertransference), "It's amazing. The group members must have been standing outside your office during supervision. We walked in prepared, knew how we were going to address the situation, and members of the group were saying the same things that we had talked about in here." It is as if the therapist walks in with a sign carrying the words, "Its okay. I am free of it (the countertransference bind), and soon you will be too."

Returning to the example of the couples group and my

removed wedding band, in this instance I "mastered" the counter-transference reaction through a series of discussions with my co-therapist and another respected colleague. (Although my co-therapist had been aware of my separation, he himself had been unaware that I had removed my wedding band; nor had I disclosed to him my own feelings of discomfort as a couples therapist. In retrospect, of course, it would have been much better had I been discussing these feelings with him right along.)

> After considerable time spent processing my feelings, I came into the group the next week feeling "prepared." I understood that my own feelings of inadequacy about myself as a marriage partner were strongly resonating with concerns that were abundant among the couples in the group. I entered the group the following week "at peace" on this issue, to be greeted by group members' expressions of surprise and amusement (tinged with regret) at the extent to which they had put the group leaders "on the spot" the previous week. They then went on to talk about how inept they felt as parents and marital partners.

Another important aspect of the resolution of this particular countertransference bind in my couples group was that it had repercussions in other aspects of my clinical work, as well. Much to my surprise, the week that the resolution occurred in my couples group, an ACOA member of my noncouples group raised the same issue, as did two of my individual patients. It turned out that the four patients who had raised the issue, as well as other members of both groups, had all noticed the removal of my wedding band several months before. When the issue was explored, some commented that they had felt confused about it — feeling unsure about what it meant, uncertain about whether there had even been a change, and uneasy about bringing it up. That it came up simultaneously with so many of my patients is an example of the kind of nonverbal "leaking" that I have been referring to. I was somehow signaling to my patients that I was now in a position to hear and to effectively deal with their concerns, and could help them process the issues that the removal of the ring had triggered in each of them.

Although I never shared information with either group or with individual patients about my change in status, exploration about their fantasies was extremely useful. Group members' reactions and fantasies varied enormously. Speculations included: (1) that there had never been a ring on that hand at all (i.e., that I'd never been married); (2) that I had an infected finger and that at some point the ring would be put back on; (3) that I was recently widowed; and (4) that I was recently separated. Emotional reactions also ranged considerably from a sincerely stated hope on the part of one group member that the missing ring did not mean anything bad for me, but that if it did, there would be a place where I could go to get the kind of help that I had given to others, to the wish of an unmarried female member that if, indeed, I was now single, I might better understand how wretched life was for *her*. Once the issue could be addressed (patients somehow understanding that I was now ready to deal with it), both their concerns about me and the resonating concerns about themselves could also be addressed.

As has been pointed out, psychotherapy groups can stir up extremely intense countertransference reactions in the therapist because many voices may be resonating with a single theme that pushes relevant buttons for the group leader as well. Such feelings can be extremely uncomfortable for the group leader. However, as the therapist moves from being stuck with a feeling that drags him down or makes him anxious, to understanding and using it, new energy is added to the group. Let us take, for example, a situation in which the leader begins to feel anxious during a session, in response to a growing sense that "the group hates me" or "they are all enraged with me." One possible way to extricate oneself from this kind of massively overpowering feeling is to "count heads," in order to see if you can feel shades of differences among the members. Thus, when the group becomes mired down with what seems to be a unified and overpowering negative transference, the group leader might ask individual members more about where each is specifically "coming from" (leading to differentiation among individual members and interruption of the overwhelming power of the negative transference). The therapist might say, for example, "Many people in here are angry. Can you tell me more about your feelings, Mr. X?" or, "In what ways are your feelings similar and different from those of Ms. Y?" Just as the group leader can enhance the group transferences by group-as-a-whole interpretations, powerful negative group transferences (and the leader's countertransference reactions) can be defused by individuating members and their reactions.

This chapter has considered countertransference in some detail because the group leader's countertransference reactions may be especially intense in ACOA therapy groups — particularly if the leader is also an ACOA. Signals of countertransference have been reviewed as well as ways of extricating oneself from countertransference impasses.

7
Leader Issues

Chapter 6 focused on leader issues involving countertransference — in a sense the most generic and pervasive leader issue. In this chapter other leader issues are addressed. However, the countertransference theme continues, as each leader issue is explored against the backdrop of the countertransference issues that are raised.

The Group Leader Who Is an ACOA

An unusual characteristic of those who treat ACOA patients is that many are, themselves, adult children of alcoholics. It is particularly important that these ACOA therapists be reflective about their motives in choosing to work with this population, and the feelings that get stirred up in the course of working with ACOA clients.

The extent to which the ACOA group leader resonates with the clinical material may be his greatest treasure in working with ACOA clients. His own resonation, however, may also get him into trouble, if not adequately examined and understood. It is important that the ACOA therapist be aware that countertransference is a part of life as a therapist, and that certain "buttons" may be especially likely to be pushed when they are related to issues that recapitulate the family drama. In this regard, the ACOA therapist's interest in doing group psychotherapy with ACOA patients is both an asset and a liability. Familiarity with the issues is helpful, as long as distance and perspective are not lost.

Wood (1987) describes, with particular clarity, some of the

dilemmas of the ACOA therapist. She points out that many ACOAs have sacrificed "a substantial portion of their selfhood in order to minister to the physical and psychic needs of their parents" — a sacrifice motivated by love and compassion for their parents, fear of losing them, and intense longing for a satisfying, sustaining relationship (p. 144). Understandably, the role of strong helper is preferable to the vulnerable role of the dependent, fearful child. Thus,

> A sizable number of these instinctive helpers choose to specialize in the treatment of chemically dependent individuals and families. They often bring to their work an extraordinary capacity for empathy, and their will to restore . . . can become the basis for the very qualities of hope, courage, and dogged perseverance that are indispensable to success in this field. (pp. 144-145)

However, as Wood also points out, this "will to restore" can become a "destructive force" when accompanied by "an impatient 'rush to recovery' by the therapist" whose own sense of emotional safety and self-esteem are dependent on the patient's progress in therapy (p. 145). In describing her work with a chemically addicted ACOA, Wood provides a particularly graphic description of her own temporary enmeshment in this kind of clinical trap. Thus, she describes how she protected her patient "from his true feelings, by experiencing them for him." She "felt the terror" and the "sense of impending disaster" that "he was determined not to feel or remember," and in so doing she "tried to wrestle his compulsion to the mat" (p. 150). Productive treatment resumed when she recognized the force of her own "will to restore" and changed course with the patient — recognizing

> . . . that in my own desperation to see Jeremy well and free of the awful feelings that fed his compulsion, I was coercing healthful solutions to self-destructive urges. Further, I had to accept that such solutions . . . communicated a fear of the dark feelings that lay beneath these urges rather than (providing) the understanding and acceptance that was necessary to assuage these feelings. Further, my panicky maneuverings indicated a lack of faith in Jeremy's ability to tolerate his feelings and work them through. (p. 151)

ACOA therapists may also, at times, have a propensity to block or dampen patients' expressions of painful feelings, since, "in the heroic therapist's family of origin, emotionality and conflict never came to a good end" (Wood, 1987, p. 146). Through Wood's discussion, we come to understand how the ACOA therapist may hinder the work of her patients by employing the same blocking maneuvers that were once used to "restore the false harmony" of her own alcoholic family (p. 154). Since, however, the goal of therapy is not to eliminate painful feelings, but to help the patient experience them in a safe context in which they can become reintegrated, the ACOA therapist needs to stay on top of her own reactions as strong feelings emerge.

In clarifying the forces at work in the ACOA therapist, Wood (1984) brings to bear the concept of "fate neurosis" (Deutsch, 1930; Wurmser, 1981). She, thus, explains the ACOA hero's "indomitable and sometimes self-destructive will to restore the alcoholic parent" by citing Wurmser's (1981) lucid comments:

> The aim (is) not to find the good parent, the idealized one; it (is) to find the severely damaged and disappointing parent, toward whom all anger and pain (are) still raging and to repair and restore him, to wipe out his peculiar damage, to undo his specific disappointments — and the greater his shortcomings, the more exciting the hope of his restoration. (cited in Wood, 1984, p. 6)

Through this mechanism the individual operates under the unconscious belief that if she can finally heal the impaired loved one, she will also heal her own damaged self — eventually to enjoy victory over past suffering.

Another potential hazard for therapists who are themselves ACOAs is that they may find themselves pulled toward the "self-help" model with concomitant pressures toward self-disclosure and sharing of personal experiences (as one might do in the role of an AA or Al-Anon sponsor). For ACOA therapists who are in Al-Anon it may, at times, be confusing as to how the role of therapist differs from or converges upon that of sponsor. But it is essential to recognize that the two roles are quite different. A sponsor continues to help himself while also helping the other. While, in the course of our work, we as therapists also continue to grow, our growth is never the focus of the therapeutic relationship; it is always the patient's growth that comes first. We need to be clear that the interventions that we make are responsive to the patients needs, rather than meeting needs of our own.

We work in a field marked by good intentions and powerful wishes to help. These are laudable — and even essential — but not enough. Well-intentioned, but poorly prepared therapists may, in fact, do more harm than good. It is essential for ACOA therapists to be self-reflective about their motives and to be aware that skill, preparation, and training are essential. Having shared the experiences of being an ACOA is far from sufficient preparation. In this regard, being effective as an ACOA therapist is clearly differentiated from effective functioning as an Al-Anon/ACOA sponsor.

Because of the potential hazards for group leaders who are themselves ACOAs (overidentification with the population, assumptions of sameness, etc.), there may be some advantage to a co-therapy team that combines one group leader who is an ACOA and one who is not. Although this is probably the ideal combination (particularly when one is a male and one is a female), this may not always be possible. To some extent, tunnel vision will be reduced by the use of *any* co-leader (even if the second is also an ACOA) since, for the most part, two leaders are less likely to get caught up in the same places and will be able to provide some distance and perspective for one another. Another alternative is the use of a non-ACOA supervisor who can help the ACOA group leader process the group material and who will tend to be less caught up in the dysfunctional family that the leader may be resonating with while in the group. Finally, countertransference supervision groups may be helpful in which several ACOA group leaders come together in a group format to process and deal with their countertransference issues around working with this population.

In one group that I supervise, a particularly clear instance of leader resonation with a group theme occurred.

This group, during the first few weeks of its formation, struggled to identify the "most problematic patient." The ACOA leader found herself, by the end of the first session, colluding with the group — feeling, with them, that a particular "problem patient" did not "fit" in the group and allowed the group to persuade this member that he did not belong. When the patient did not return the following week, the leader expressed relief, stating in supervision "that the group would be better off without this patient, who was too sick." The leader's own wish to "save the family" by "ridding it of its troubled member" — a dynamic that she was all too familiar with — blinded

her to the realization of what the group (and she) was reenacting. Instead, she colluded with them and helped this "unfit" patient leave the group, thus recapitulating the family fantasy that everything would be fine if only the problem member were removed. A few weeks later the group took up the same cause again, searching anew for a problem patient to eliminate. At this point, the leader, understanding her own earlier collusion, was able to intervene more effectively and this time helped the group retain and work with the new problem patient that it had identified.

Other Personal Issues in the Life of the Therapist

It is likely that the therapist's personal life experiences and conflicts may resonate along a number of directions with those of the patients that he treats. As Kanfer and Schefft (1988) point out, "Significant life experiences that have strong emotional valences make the therapist particularly vulnerable to reacting on the basis of her own needs rather than those of the client" (p. 374). It is thus important for the therapist to be aware of sensitive or unsettled personal areas and to pay special attention when working with patients who are struggling with similar issues. For example, a therapist who is recently divorced or separated may need to exercise special caution in treating patients whose central presenting issues involve marital discord. Similarly, an ACOA therapist who has recently succeeded in getting his alcoholic father into treatment may need to pay special attention to his reactions to a patient whose alcoholic parents are still abusively drinking.

When working with patients whose issues resonate with the therapist's, blurring of boundaries is more likely. It is thus important that the therapist be clear about the ground rules and, when one of them is about to be broken, make a conscious and thoughtful decision that such a modification is in the patient's best interest. As discussed in Chapter 6, when rules get broken without any active decision on the part of the therapist, we can usually infer that countertransference issues are being stirred up (and that the therapist's behavior may not, in fact, be in the patient's best interest). A blurred sense on the part of the therapist about how to conduct a particular course of therapy may contribute to constant

testing by the patient to discover what is acceptable (while, meanwhile, the therapist is also trying to discover what will and will not be effective within the therapeutic agreement). As Langs (1975) succinctly states,

> Many deviations and techniques are not undertaken primarily because of the patient's needs, but are rationalizations of the extensive countertransference gratifications they offer the psychotherapist. In so doing, therapists neglect the ego-strengthening factors . . . inherent in the firm maintenance of proper and clearcut boundaries and ground rules . . . and [the] disruptive aspects inherent in the therapist's failure to maintain these much-needed boundaries. (p. 117)

In addition to paying special attention to the operating ground rules and modifications that may be introduced, the therapist concerned about the impact of her own personal issues on her clinical work may need to seek out additional support or consultation (through personal therapy or supervision). If complications remain and the therapist continues to feel that her own reactions are getting in the way of a particular patient's therapeutic growth, referral to another therapist should be considered.

Selecting a Supervisor

It is important to select a supervisor who you feel will "stretch" your clinical potential, and who you respect and look up to. Equally important, however, is that you pick someone with whom you feel comfortable and with whom you feel you can establish a solid working alliance. As Kanfer and Schefft (1988) state,

> An open relationship that fosters the frank discussion of sensitive topics between supervisor and student is essential in establishing a favorable atmosphere for learning. In fact, the supervisory experience is a change process, not unlike therapy itself. (p. 368)

Supervision should also be interesting and fun, not anxiety-provoking and intimidating. There is no more reason for you not to have fun, or to enjoy the supervision, than there is for your patients not to enjoy their work with you. Just as it is possible for the group therapist to be playful at times, and to laugh appreciatively in the group, it is equally possible to laugh together in supervision.

Most therapists (and their supervisors) do find joy in their work or they would probably not continue. However, they may be reluctant to allow themselves to appreciate this. We have all experienced the joy of getting to know another, as well as the pleasure of helping patients to experience that joy. There is clearly pleasure in seeing others make headway and feeling that we have been helpful. There is joy in sharing a touching moment and pleasure in feeling close. As therapists, it is important that we are able to be in touch with this joy as it emerges in the group, and again, as we reprocess our experiences with a senior supervisor or in peer supervision.

The spirit of fun is essential to the work of the group therapist. As Searles (1979) states, "the patient benefits most from our sharing of humorous, playful moments together" (p. 85). Learning about ourselves in therapy does not have to be a heavy and ponderous experience. The group therapist should feel free to laugh when patients share something funny, and should find a supervisor who can do this as well. For example, after a particularly heavy session, a patient shared an amusing self-reflection as he headed to the door. I chuckled, and he said, "I'm glad you can still find some humor in my situation. It's a relief to me to know that it's not all that grim."

In either peer supervision or working with a senior supervisor, it is also important to be able to share successful cases and special moments in the therapeutic process that you are particularly proud of, as well as creative interventions that work. It is important that your collegial exchanges allow you the opportunity to think creatively, within the framework in which you operate. By allowing yourself in supervision to share successes as well as failures — strengths as well as weaknesses — you will be in a better position to encourage group members to do the same.

A final cautionary word about supervision is in order. Supervision provides a rich arena not only for processing and sorting out what is going on in the group, but also for exploring your own personal reactions to group members. Understanding your countertransference feelings — both objective and subjective, will contribute substantially to the quality and depth of your clinical work. Particularly when countertransference feelings are intense, there may be a temptation on the part of either supervisor or supervisee to blur the boundaries between supervision and psychotherapy. However, as Kanfer and Schefft (1988) clearly state, "both supervisor and student must be careful not to violate the structure and purpose of supervision" (p. 370). The focus of the work in a supervisory hour should be on understanding what is going on in the therapist, as a way of better understanding the dynamics of his patients and of his group. When the therapists' own conflicts need addressing, therapy, in addition to supervision, should be sought.

Choosing Between Supervision and Psychotherapy

Throughout this text, I have highlighted the importance of the therapist's ability to stay on top of countertransference reactions and, in general, to be appropriately self-aware and reflective about the course of the therapy and his work with the patient. Supervision — whether it be peer supervision, or supervision with a senior therapist, individually or in a supervision group — can be very helpful for this purpose.

At times, however, the therapist may need additional help. Most psychodynamically oriented therapists will have been in psychotherapy at some point during their professional careers (usually toward the beginning of their careers, and often extending for several years). Often there is a feeling that through these therapy experiences our own "adult-child" issues have been adequately processed. However, therapists frequently find when working with certain kinds of patients later on in their lives, that many of the issues that they thought had been put to rest are reawakened; this is particularly a possibility for the ACOA therapist working with ACOA clients.

Although the case for returning to psychotherapy, in conjunction with (or instead of) supervision, cannot be simply stated, a few guidelines might be the following. Psychotherapy might be indicated if countertransference slippage around rules and expectations seem to be occurring with many of your patients. Often this is accompanied by a feeling of being "out of control" and "stirred up" by your work. (You may notice that you are spending more and more time worrying about your patients — or about your own behavior with them.) Another signpost that therapy may be indicated is finding yourself, as you listen to your patients, slipping into thoughts about your *own* past, or about your own present difficulties. When this occurs, it is apparent that the patient's material is triggering so much inside of you, that it becomes difficult for you to stay with the patient.

Occasionally, senior therapists react to the idea of returning to therapy by feeling that this implies that they have "regressed" in some way. I believe that this is rarely the case. All of us continue to rework important issues from the past throughout our lives. With each new stage of our own development — as we take on new patient populations, as we try out new kinds of professional activities — we have an opportunity to rework important issues from the past.

The Therapist's Motives: On Countertransference Goodness and Availability

As therapists it is important to be aware of how we have gotten into the work that we do and what we expect of ourselves. As Searles (1979) points out, "We originally entered this profession in an unconscious effort to assuage our guilt . . . over having failed to cure our parents" (p. 28). Many therapists, and perhaps especially so those who are themselves ACOAs, believe that they should always be able to "stretch themselves a little bit further" — extending themselves yet a little bit more. How often we hear of patients who call at late hours of the night or on weekends and who get extra time between sessions as a sort of "unofficial therapy." It is important that the ACOA therapist think of these as outside *sessions* — and just as important as the "official" sessions that the patient has planned (and paid for). If the therapist does not think of these as additional "sessions" with his patient, he should ask himself why not. He may also consider setting up contracts with patients about additional contacts that occur outside the usual hour: (1) charging for these extra sessions; (2)

putting limits on them; and (3) offering additional planned sessions when it appears that the usual frequency is not adequate.

As one ACOA therapist that I supervised put it, "I feel that I am making a living as a therapist during the hours that I see patients in their official appointments. However, it feels more like 'doing God's work' (does this need to be free?) by being infinitely able to pick up the pieces at odd hours of the day or night or on weekends." For this therapist the "real test" was to be able to soothe her patients at times of unpredictability and chaos. However, as Searles (1979) points out,

> . . . we see that the kind of therapist devotion characteristic of such . . . situations is a genuinely "selfless" devotion, but selfless in a sense that is, in the long run, precisely antitherapeutic. . . . Such "devotion," . . . inevitably must be revealed, one day, as a lie. This disillusioning discovery, now, that the therapist after all is a separate person with a self of his own and self-interest of his own, after the patient has been led for so long to assume otherwise, will repeat, for the patient, his bitter childhood experience that . . . people are only interested in themselves. (pp. 86-87)

The therapist's issues around being infinitely available are especially likely to be stirred up when working with suicidal or impulsive patients. When such patients ask, "Will you be available if I need you before our next session," I have found it useful to indicate that while I do make an effort to be available for emergencies, I do not carry a beeper and am not, in reality, available and reachable at all times. This means that the patient needs to have knowledge of other emergency resources, and needs to feel free to use these when I am not available. Not only is it potentially disappointing and even dangerous to the patient to make unrealistic promises of availability, it can also be very hazardous to the health and well being of the therapist. Information on resources such as 24-hour hot lines, suicide prevention centers, and local crisis units should be given to the worried patient, along with some guidelines as to when it might be advisable to use one of these resources, rather than first trying to reach the therapist.

The therapist who reacts to a needy and demanding patient by feeling that he has to "give just a little bit more" may fail to set adequate boundaries around his private time. By so doing he does not help his patients learn how to contain out-of-control feelings. Moreover, endless gratification of the patient's demands may communicate to the patient that even his excessive needs can be met and that no change in his behavior is required to meet the demands of reality (Chu, 1988). Worse yet, patients who continue to barrage the therapist during off hours and wee hours of the night frequently get frightened about the damaging potential of their neediness and rage. That is, such patients come to fear that they may "use up" or "drive away" the therapist, thereby destroying the safe "frame" that they long for and which could contain them (if the therapist helped with this.) It is thus important to give our patients the message, "I'm not going to let you use me up." Patients need boundaries to know that they are safe, even though they may need to test the boundaries occasionally by pushing up against them.

The message must be clearly communicated that impulses can be contained and talked about in the therapy session, and that the therapist will provide a predictable structure to do this. It needs to be *safe* for the patient to bring his crisis to the therapy group. A nice example recently came to my attention of a therapist who helped to bind or "contain" her patient's rageful impulses between sessions in a manner that also protected the boundaries of the therapy relationship.

> *The therapist was treating an ACOA with self-destructive impulses, which took the form of self-mutilation with the mat cutting knives used in her photography studio. The therapist instructed her patient, when these impulses came upon her, to gather all the knives and put them in a cardboard box which she should then tape around the edges, wrap with brown paper, and, finally, retape and tie. The bound box containing the destructive implements was then to be brought to the next group therapy session, where the impulses would be discussed.*

What this therapist was very cleverly helping her patient to do was to concretely "contain" her impulses by wrapping up the dangerous implements. The therapist thereby conveyed that the dangerous impulses could be safely talked about in the next therapy session where they would no longer pose danger to the patient. The therapist was also, appropriately, expecting the patient to assume some of the responsibility for her treatment and for her own safety.

In addition to the benefits (both for the patient and the therapist) of clear limit setting by the therapist, there is an extra bonus, both for the patient directly involved and also for the other members of the group. For patients who find it impossible to consider their own needs and to say "no" to others, the therapist can serve as a valuable role model by declining the role of omnipotent provider. The opposite is, of course, also true; and consequently, when we extend ourselves beyond our own reasonable limits, we need to be aware of the message that this gives to our overgiving patients.

Often related to our overextending ourselves are feelings that we have about looking "fair," "nice," "kind," or "generous." Although to some extent such feelings are common to all of us, we may want to explore them further if they assume excessive importance. Are we motivated by the wish to give a reparative experience or perhaps the desire to feel good about ourselves? While neither of these motives is necessarily inappropriate in our work as therapists, they are also rarely sufficient.

Moore (1965), in discussing the nurturant needs of the therapist in working with alcoholic patients, captures an aspect of countertransference that is equally appropriate in our work with ACOAs.

> Being therapeutically inclined, we have a heightened need to be nurturant and giving people. We are personally gratified by patients and clients who see us as nurturant and gratifying and who repay us with affection and thankfulness. We are not so gratified by patients who are less affectionate or thankful. We try very hard to give as much as we can . . . and discover to our dismay that this is never enough; in fact the more we give the more is expected . . . It is hard for us to get our own infantile gratifications . . . when working with the addicted person. We may find ourselves encouraging those traits of dependency . . . which will give us some of this gratification and discouraging those little signs of maturity . . . (pp. 41-42)

It is clear that we cannot afford to be unselfconscious and unreflective about our behaviors. We need to be responsive to our guts and at the some time guided by our heads. This is not to be understood as encouragement to act on "gut reactions" but, rather, for therapists to pay attention to their own feelings as a mechanism for *understanding* what is going on, and responding thoughtfully and therapeutically.

Therapist Transparency and Self-Disclosure

Therapists frequently feel pressured when patients raise questions and concerns about personal aspects of the therapists' lives — on the surface, requests for "facts" about the therapist. Those requests that seem to have the most legitimacy (and the ones that therapists often feel the most pressured to respond to) are those that bear directly on the presenting issue that the patient wishes to work on. For example, in an ACOA group, the question of whether the therapist is herself an ACOA; in a recovery group, whether the therapist is a recovering alcoholic; in a couples group, whether the therapist is herself married or coupled. Yet, other questions are often equally important to the patient — for example, how experienced is the therapist? It is important to recognize that simple "straightforward" responses may not, in fact, be responsive to the concerns that are being raised by such questions. What is generally being raised is a wish for reassurance that the therapist will have the appropriate credentials to help the patient with his areas of concern.

Let us examine, for example, the question to the couples therapist, "Are you married?" Though not stated, what is generally of interest in such a question is not simply whether or not the therapist is married, but whether his personal experience has been adequate to effectively deal with the relationship problems that the patient presents. (A successful marriage might well be a credential — but would 10 years of strained, impoverished relating, even if one were still with the same partner?) Since in most instances what the patient is requesting is reassurance that the therapist will be able to help, what is most important in handling these questions is not the precise answer that is given — or even whether or not a specific answer is given — but how the question is handled. In general, in my experience, when therapists are uncomfortable with a question (often because the patient's doubts resonate with their own) they either rush in too quickly to answer the question or in some way convey defensiveness. Generally, these responses are motivated by resonating countertransference feelings in the therapist — that is, his own concerns about his level of expertise, credentials, and ability, ultimately, to help.

A brief clinical vignette will help illustrate what I am getting at.

> Not long ago, a new group leader in our clinic, who had just graduated from social work school, was "initiated" by her group, on the night that she entered, with the question, "Are you still a trainee?" The new young leader, vastly relieved to be past her training, responded, "No, I finished my training in June." Although to group members the young therapist's response may not have felt quite as reassuring as the new co-leader had hoped, what was more important was that she had shown her lack of experience by hastily answering the question, without doing anything to process its underlying meaning. The group members, by this time quite sophisticated about the workings of a group, responded by informing her, "Our therapists don't usually answer questions like that."

As this example illustrates, patients often need reassurance about the therapist's skill and ability to handle problems in areas that are also conflictual for the therapist. Understanding what the questions trigger in the therapist is essential to adequate handling of the patient's concerns. In addition, I have found it useful in my own practice to have a basic policy about self-disclosure, which I explain to patients whenever personal questions come up. What I generally say to patients when they ask a personal question about me is the following: "Generally, I do not find it useful to share personal information about myself. However, I'd be interested in knowing more about how this particular question might be important to you, and how a given answer of one sort or another might be useful." Implicit in my statement is a suggestion that together, the patient and I will consider whether a modification in my policy might be useful in this particular instance. I generally find that patients are comforted by the knowledge that I'm willing to explore the issue, and perhaps comforted most of all by understanding that there are thoughtful ground rules guiding my work. Almost inevitably, these discussions eventuate in a clarification of the patient's concerns about whether I will be able to understand and help with the important work which he has come to tackle.

Co-Leadership

Benefits and Costs

Co-leadership offers a number of special benefits both to the group leaders and to the group members. Leaders gain from the opportunity to have peer support during the group itself, and to have easy access to backup coverage for holidays and vacations. In addition, the prospect of sharing the rich and fascinating experience of group life makes it even more fun. Leaders also benefit, in terms of their own growth as therapists, by having an opportunity to watch another therapist work. The sharing of responsibility and the decreased sense of burden that often accompanies this, as well as the ability to give constructive feedback to one another, help leaders to stay on top of the intricate, and sometimes confusing, dynamics of the group.

From the perspective of group members, benefits include the opportunity to watch functional, adaptive behavior in the co-leader pair — a real bonus for many patients from dysfunctional families, who have had little opportunity to observe open dyadic communication and sharing of responsibility. In addition, particularly with a male/female co-therapy team, co-leadership enhances the "re-creation of the family" and the group's capacity to fully play out the many dimensions of family transference. Co-leadership for many patients may also diffuse the transference (particularly feelings around dependency and loss) since there is not just a single "parent" to rely on. Finally, co-leadership provides an opportunity for two pairs of eyes to view the situation rather than one, and for the patients to benefit from the leaders' collaboration.

Along with the many benefits of co-leadership, however, there are also some important costs which need to be considered. In private practice, co-leadership is generally less financially rewarding for the therapist, since it is rare to charge patients twice as much for having two leaders. In addition, extra time needs to be allowed after each group session to process the group material with one another and to discuss future interventions and clinical strategies. Finally, co-therapy adds an additional leader responsibility since the leaders must take the time to attend to their own relationship. They must be prepared to talk about what is going on between them, to explore differences, to deal with attractions to one another without acting on them, and to be open to understanding how issues that come up between them may be reflected in the work of the group.

The importance of monitoring the relationship between the co-leaders cannot be underestimated. Group members will be sensitive to tensions between the leaders, just as children are ever sensitive to tensions between their parents. Even when the group does not directly address these issues, they inadvertently get played out in the group, and if the leaders are discerning, they will ultimately "hear" the material and be able to process it with the group.

An example of group resonation of a significant, but unprocessed, co-leader interaction occurred in a group that I supervised for many years.

> The two co-therapists had worked together for more than five years and were very attached to each other and as well as to the group. In supervision, they would occasionally joke about "their family" and when they disagreed or quarreled (usually playfully) in supervision, they would sometimes turn to me and ask how I liked "doing couples therapy." Throughout the first four years of our work together, the group had been a lively and productive arena for many patients' growth. Membership had been very stable — nearly all members staying in excess of two years — with terminations well planned and processed by the group. In the middle of the fourth year, Dr. A, the female co-therapist, adopted her first child. She took off from the group for four weeks, and returned both jubilant and exhausted. For the next six months, still somewhat sleep deprived, she "faded out" periodically throughout the group. Although she never actually fell asleep, the male co-therapist was "constantly on guard and aware of trying to keep her attention — changing positions, coughing, etc., — to make sure that we wouldn't lose her." None of this came up in the supervision until it had been going on for nearly six months. At that point group members began to talk about how "nonconfronting" members always seemed to be to one another lately, and pointed to the

tendency of group members to "walk on egg shells with one another." They compared this to "old times" in the group, when
things were "more vibrant," and described the present group as
"nice, but engaged in less productive work than it had been in the
past." Upon hearing this, and having, myself, noticed the female
co-therapist's "sleepiness" in the supervision, I asked if anything
similar to what the group was describing might be being played out
between the two co-therapists. The male therapist blushed and
acknowledged that maybe he had been a little "too nice" for the
past six months, fearing to hurt Dr. A's feelings by pointing out her
tendency to "fade out." Dr. A was totally surprised both by the
feedback that she had been looking drowsy and about her co-
therapist's discomfort with her.

When we explored further, what emerged was that the male
therapist had not only been protecting Dr. A by withholding his
observations, but more importantly had been protecting *himself.*
Upon reflection, he realized that with the arrival of Dr. A's child, he
became aware that she now had another family that took pre-
cedence over the one that he and she shared. He felt, too, that her
drowsiness was a constant reminder that her energy was elsewhere;
and, already feeling "less important to her than before," he was
feeling too vulnerable in the co-therapy relationship to confront her
about her behavior. After talking about this in supervision, things
began to perk up in the group — and even though Dr. A continued
to occasionally look as if she might "nod off" in the group, the
group itself became more lively and confrontational. It became clear
that what the group was picking up was not only Dr. A's sleepiness,
but perhaps even more important, the careful, less engaged, less
open interaction that had developed between the co-therapy pair.

In subsequent weeks both of the leaders began to listen actively to
material, and to openly process with the group material relevant to
the leaders' "remiss" behavior — both the drowsiness and the male
leader's failure to call attention to it. Patients' feelings about both
leaders' clinical negligence were slow in coming forth but, ultimately, productively explored. Highly conflictual feelings emerged
regarding group members' perceptions that the leaders had "erred."
Powerful wishes to see the leaders as the idealized, perfect, infallible
parent figures, long yearned for, were set against equally powerful
wishes to see them as human and more "real." Competitive feelings
were also productively explored, as group members talked about
the therapists' mistakes as, in some way, giving members a bit of a
"leg up."

Choosing a Co-Leader

In choosing a co-leader a balance must be struck between comfortable similarities and profitable differences between the two leaders. Although many combinations are possible and workable, differences among the leaders (as long as they are within a comfortable range) can provide richness for the group. For this reason, I prefer male-female combinations whenever possible, and personal and stylistic differences within a range that the leaders can comfortably tolerate. What are probably the most important criteria are that the leaders generally like and respect one another, look forward to working together, and anticipate that their work will be both fun and rewarding.

If after meeting a potential co-leader you have any reservations about your comfort in working together, this should be discussed at length, prior to making a commitment to co-leadership. Counterindications for a co-therapy pair include the following: (1) differences in clinical orientation which leaders believe will be conflictual (for example, one leader who is very traditionally trained and analytically oriented, and another whose training is in transactional analysis, or gestalt therapy); (2) tremendous disparity in activity level, which the leaders may already know about from their contacts with one another outside the group (for example, one leader is extremely active, emotional, and affectively available, and the other is extremely reserved and finds high activity and emotionality irksome); (3) negative attraction between the two group leaders (for example, when two group leaders find themselves disliking one another or find the other unappealing personally); (4) uncomfortable positive attraction (for example, when one or both of the leaders have had thoughts of dating the other or of having an affair — unless they can comfortably give up acting on these wishes); and (5) a negative history together that one or both leaders cannot get past.

Although many group therapists believe that co-leadership also requires that the leaders are nearly coequal in status, in my own experience, supervising more than 150 co-leader pairs over the last fifteen years,* I believe that status "equality" is nearly

*Some 70 of these pairs were together for a year or more in long term groups, another 80 in short term (5-week) groups.

impossible to achieve, and that a considerable amount of inequality can be managed as long as the leaders are aware of the differences (and the implications for their work together), and are receptive to processing this as "grist for the mill" in the group and in supervision. Considering the many possible status differentials among people, it is hard to imagine a truly coequal pair (and certainly not "coequal" in the eyes of all group members, since each will have his own yardstick to use for measuring equality). The perceived status of various professional disciplines differ; age carries with it differential status since it is often associated with different amounts of experience; experience levels may vary independently of age (and also independent of number of years of actual work in the field); maleness and femaleness may carry differential status for some members (and also for some leaders) and so on. Particularly in long-term groups which go on for years, and in which there is co-leader turnover, the newer leader will almost always be perceived as having a lower status than the one who has been there longer. In my experience, nearly every group has a "big C" (the more senior co-leader) and a "little c" (the less senior co-leader). In our clinic, in fact, such an arrangement helps provide training for group leaders beginning their work in this field. What is important is that the status differentials among the leaders are not uncomfortable for them, that they can listen for issues related to these differences, and deal with them appropriately when they come up in the group, and that the leaders make every effort to divide the work load of the group as evenly as possible. Despite status differentials (actual or perceived), the work load can and should be shared, and impediments to this (for example, the senior leader having difficulty sharing his group with a new co-leader) should be discussed.

Processing and Understanding Co-Therapy Conflicts

Our understanding of countertransference dynamics — and, in particular, the ways in which the therapist becomes a "container" (Bion, 1962) for important, conflictual feelings in the group — can be applied to the co-therapy team as a unit. Thus, when conflicts emerge between the two group leaders, it may be fruitful to examine the possibility that the co-therapist unit is experiencing two sides of a conflict — with one part being experienced by one therapist, and the other part by the other. (That is, that the group is "impressing" one part of the conflict on one member of the co-therapy team, and another part on the other.) As discussed in Chapter 6, in the course of therapy, certain of the patients' unacceptable feelings may get projected out and "contained" by the group leader, whose resonation with the material, and ability to understand what he is experiencing, makes it possible for him to "digest it" and put it back out for the group, or individual group members, to use. This occurs in a similar fashion within the co-leader dyad. Whereas with one leader, the patient (or group) puts out a part of the conflict so that it will be externalized (and experienced as a struggle with the leader), with two leaders, the group (or given patient) has an opportunity to externalize *both* parts of the conflict — leaving the leaders to represent the polarities, and to "fight it out among themselves," (with the group members freed up to "observe the conflict").

It is essential that the leaders in this situation use their understanding of the conflict between *themselves* as a way to better understand the feuding, intrapsychic positions within the group (and within individual members). These moments of tension, when the leaders experience conflict between themselves, can be important turning points, if the leaders use their understanding of the conflict between themselves as a way of better gauging what is going on in the group. Of course, the obverse of this is also true. That is, when tension remains within the co-leader team, it interferes with the progress of the group, often serving as a major distraction (for group members, as well as for the leaders). It is one of the greatest challenges of co-leadership to be able to understand and use the dyadic conflicts that emerge. Good supervision, or at least consultation with a respected colleague, is essential during these periods of conflict.

This chapter has focused on those leader issues that substantially influence the group therapist's effectiveness. The next chapter examines treatment techniques that the leader may use to increase his effectiveness.

8
Leader Techniques

A central task of therapy is to help the patient better understand his feelings, thoughts, and wishes and how these affect his relationships with others and his ability to achieve his goals. The group leader must be skilled at joining or allying with group members to promote an atmosphere in which this understanding can emerge. The techniques discussed in this chapter reflect some of the ways that I have found useful for establishing the treatment alliance and for enlisting group members' participation in the therapeutic journey.

Viewing Therapy as a Journey in Which "Curiosity" Is the Guide

Therapy is a journey that the patient and therapist share, in which there is a quest for knowledge and an attempt to explore and investigate new paths together. Since the therapist does not want to go on such a journey with a patient who keeps his eyes closed, the therapist's task is to enlist the patient to *look around* with him. Thus, the therapist's task is to get the patient interested or curious in looking for clues and signs along the way. The therapist may encourage this by asking questions such as, "Are you curious about that?" If the patient says "No," the therapist might ask, "How come?" or, "Ever wondered about why you weren't curious about this kind of thing, given that it happens so often and seems to get you into such fixes?" Or the therapist might ask, "Is it curious to you that you haven't been at all curious about it?"

Alternatively, the therapist may raise the patient's curiosity about a long held belief, framing it as a "notion" — implying that this idea may not be as factual as the patient might have believed. In other words, the therapist may translate a "fact" which has the quality of being a dead-end, non-negotiable issue into a "notion" worthy of exploration. Thus, the therapist might ask, "Where did you get the notion that . . . ?"

Empathy and Therapeutic Attunement

The skilled group leader gauges the appropriateness of his interventions with one hand on the pulse of the group and the other on the pulse of his alliance with individual members. The group leader is considering for each individual patient, as well as for the group as a whole, what to interpret, when, and how this will be done. As Cooper (1988) suggests, empathic attunement of the therapist is facilitated by his asking himself, "How would I be feeling now?" and, "How would I feel if somebody said this (whatever we have in mind to say) to me?" (p. 4).

Therapeutic attunement is fostered by a self-reflective, "curious" stance that is shared by both the patient and therapist. Searles' (1979) notion that inside every patient lives a therapist is appealing in this regard. It captures the driving force in all of us to know and to understand — to be able to stand back and look with perspective on what is going on inside. It is our task as therapists to help foster this stance in our patients. Perhaps we can also infer that inside every therapist lives a patient — the part of us that pushes "not to see what's going on," to keep us in the dark and unaware of our own dynamics in relationship to the patients that we are treating. Thus, it is our task not only to help the patient maintain a consistently self-reflective pose, but to maintain that stance with regard to our own work as well. Both what we do and what we do not do, what we give and what we withhold, deserve scrutiny.

Promoting Self-Evaluation

A self-reflective stance in the patient is facilitated by a therapist who helps the patient to evaluate for *himself* both what is going on and what it may mean. As Kanfer and Schefft (1988) clearly state, the therapist's role is to help "the client to evaluate and make value judgments but (he) does not do it for her" (p. 102). Accordingly, they advise therapists to

> Guide the client so that any conclusions about an action and its consequences or the evaluation of a situation is generated by the client and not you. (p. 341)

Because many people from dysfunctional families find it difficult to rely on their own internal evaluations, both about how they feel and how they are doing, an important leader task with this population is to promote self-evaluation. Thus, it is helpful for leaders to make interventions that will help the patient to assess for herself how she is doing and the progress that she is making.

For example, a patient who feels that her presentation to others is always incompetent and bumbling might be asked at the end of a group session, in which she has expressed herself well and has connected to other members, "Jill, how do you feel about your participation in the group this evening?" Leaders might further ask Jill how she felt about how she presented herself to others and how she felt about the responses that she got back. Other members might also be asked to give their impression of Jill's involvement in the group that evening. Often, this is a more useful and, in the long run, more change-promoting intervention than a more direct leader appraisal such as, "You seem to be coming across very clearly tonight, Jill."

Another example might be a patient who has been avoiding discussion of an important issue (e.g., a patient who will be having major surgery in two weeks and has known about it for the past four weeks but has not been processing it in the group). The therapist might be tempted to ask the patient why she hadn't been talking about her upcoming surgery. It might be more productive instead to comment, "I wonder if you have had any thoughts, Martha, about the fact that you're going to be having a very serious operation in a couple of weeks but haven't been talking about it in here." While a "why" question may lead the patient to feel defensive, as if she has to somehow rationalize her failure to communicate, the latter question, we would hope, would help the patient to take a more self-reflective stance. The message that we would want the patient to have is that we are interested in her thoughts about what has gotten in the way. It is the *obstacles* that are important and interesting for us to take a look at. Basically, what we want to do with our patients is to help them develop a reflective, curious posture. As discussed earlier, sometimes it is even appropriate to ask patients whether they have been "curious" about a particular behavior (and if *not*, whether it is curious at all to them that they haven't even been curious about it?) For example, we might say, "Martha, you're having some surgery in two weeks and have barely mentioned it. Have you wondered at all about what's been going on that has prevented you from bringing it up in the group?"

Encouraging patients to be able to judge for themselves how they are doing and the progress that they are making is also useful with regard to interventions about outside-of-group successes. As therapists, understandably, we are often very proud of our patients when they succeed. (Sometimes we even view this as a way of measuring our own success.) The patient's knowledge that his therapist is proud of him is by no means information that must be "hidden" from the patient; however, it should not be the primary focus. Perhaps, to state the obvious, it is the patient's feelings that are important — and should remain so — not the therapist's.

It is also important to remember that events that are *outwardly* unambiguous "successes" may be perceived ambivalently by the patient. A therapist who jumps in too hastily to compliment or congratulate may miss an important opportunity to explore the meaning of an event with the patient. Let us take, for example, a 27-year-old patient who has been living at home with his alcoholic parents — unable to separate from his highly enmeshed family. After months of screening potential housemates he has finally arranged a living situation that is far better than anything that he had hoped for. The therapist might be inclined to respond enthusiastically with something like, "John that's wonderful!" However, a more cautious, and potentially more productive, comment might be, "How does it feel to see yourself having gotten to this point?" Or the therapist might start out with a comment such as, "It must feel good to have been accepted by the two new housemates." (Even here the language is in terms of how it feels to the patient, rather than to the therapist.) This might be followed up with an inquiry about additional feelings that the patient may have had. It is important for us to remember that even successes may not be unambivalently joyful experiences. Patients may feel anxious about the fact that things will be different and worried about the loss of what has become familiar. They may also be fearful of failure, or fearful that supports that have been available when they were not doing so well may vanish now that they are moving ahead. It is important that the therapist leave room for this kind of exploration.

Phrasing Questions to Maximize Group Processing

At times, leader's comments to the group (interpretations or clarifications) are intended not so much to further current discussion but, rather, to be slowly metabolized by the group for use in future work. When, however, the intention of the leader's comment is to carry the discussion further, or to explore more thoroughly underlying feelings, thoughts, and fantasies, it is useful to avoid questions that simply lead to yes/no answers and to phrase questions, instead, in a way that will lead to fuller responses. In general, questions that begin with "how" or "in what way" are generally more useful for this purpose than questions that begin with "why" or "do you" or "are you," which are more likely to lead to simple yes/no answers.

Keeping in mind that the task of the leader is to help the group to process and explore, it may also be useful for us to consider again the difference between a dynamically oriented therapy group and an education group. While both experiences are educative in nature, the goal of the therapy group is not specifically to provide information or to evaluate members' behaviors. In a therapy group, the goal is to help patients *process* each member's experiences and ongoing events within the group. Although gathering of information and receiving evaluative feedback will occur within the context of the therapy group, the goal is to help patients learn to do this for themselves and for one another in the group.

Particularly when the group is stuck, anxious, or seems to be in need of leader assistance, leaders are often tempted to step into the "teacher mode," more appropriate for an education group or classroom situation, and temporarily leave behind their group facilitator function. This is understandable, since the classroom is the most familiar group context for both members and leaders, and at times of stress leaders may fall back on their many years of classroom experience. The other didactic mode that leaders some-times fall into during stressful periods in the group is the "mother role" — again understandably regressing to the familiar "fix-it" position with which we have all had a great deal of experience (either as the recipient or as the fixer). However, as Winnicott (1965) admonishes, emphasizing the importance of the therapist remaining "professionally involved," the therapist "is not a res-cuer, a teacher, an ally, or a moralist" (p. 162). Mother/teacher-tone questions (as differentiated from questions that encourage the patient to process for himself what is going on) might include: (1) "John, do you think that is really a good idea?" or, (2) a statement such as, "What you need to do is. . . ."

A more neutral position that alerts the patient to consider and reflect upon his options might be expressed by commenting: (1) "What thoughts did you have about how that might work for you?" "Has it worked out in the past?" or, (2) "What would it be like for you if you did do such and such?" What distinguishes the mother/teacher mode from the facilitator/leader mode is that ques-tions and statements are framed in such a way as to leave the patient in a position to continue to process his experience. Ques-tions are neither closed-ended suggestions nor closed-ended mes-sages not to proceed; rather, they encourage the patient to contin-ue to explore what his options are, and what various choices might mean to him.

Although asking questions is an important part of the group leader's task, patients often comment that they feel "put on the spot" by therapists' questions. They re-experience the anxiety of the classroom, feeling that a particular answer is expected and that they must produce what they imagine their therapist is looking for. Though to some extent this is inevitable (and, itself, an issue to be explored), questions can often be rendered more palatable if they have an open, invitational style, which conveys genuine curiosity and interest.

It should be noted that exploration of process and promotion of self-evaluation through a curious/questioning style, while important, may need to be temporarily abridged or abandoned when a patient actively poses a threat to himself or others. Under such circumstances, it is often essential for the therapist to assume "a highly directive role, taking charge of the treatment situation" (Kanfer & Schefft, 1988, p. 353), and giving specific feedback (and evaluation) to the patient involved, along with clearly stated recommendations/plans for protecting the patient against his destructive impulses.

Making Interpretations More Palatable

Although it goes without saying that as therapists we aim to clearly communicate with our patients, there are times when the message may be more effectively delivered by something *less* than our most clever and precise articulation. Epstein (1979) alludes to this, stating:

> . . . I find that it sometimes helps matters if the patient has the feeling that I may not be having the easiest time in understanding him. . . . What this does is create a more favorable distribution of good and bad parts and of power. All badness and inferiority is no longer all within the patient; nor is all goodness and superiority within me. He feels more comfortable with me as a person who is more like himself. (pp. 268-269)

In a similar vein, a favorite mentor of mine, Alfred Stanton, used to say, "The perfect interpretation is not one which stuns the patient with our brilliance (and possibly humiliates him into wondering why he hadn't thought of it) but one which gently and slowly is spun out with the patient." He used to point out that his best interpretations were those that he stuttered out in clumsy fashion with the help of his patients, who chewed on them, clarified them, and presented them back in metabolized form. In group therapy, too, I often find it useful to mumble through important interpretations, using my own confusion (and the need to get the matter sorted out) as a technique. When I feel this will be useful, I am likely to present my thoughts quite loosely, and often haltingly, encouraging group members' active involvement in clarifying and refining.

There are also times when I make what I think is a clear statement or interpretation which leads to a confused reaction on the part of the patient, who has been unable to "digest" what I have put forth. I generally respond to the patient's confusion with a comment such as, "I don't think I've put that very clearly." Or, "that really was kind of confusing, wasn't it?" I then engage other members of the group in trying to sort out what it was that I was trying to say, and to say it "better" for me.

Another set of strategies is often necessary to make interpretations or clarifications more palatable when their content runs counter to what the patient is consciously experiencing. When the therapist wishes to make an interpretation or clarification that seemingly contradicts the feelings or thoughts that have just been expressed by the patient, it is often helpful first to show understanding and acceptance of the position that the patient has already taken, and then to proceed to add an additional perspective. Let us take, for example, a patient who reports feeling "really hurt," following abusive and humiliating treatment by his boss. This response, while possibly reflecting some part of his feelings, in all likelihood also defends against the more unacceptable feelings of anger. The therapist, interested in exploring the full range of feeling, might say, "You were aware of feeling really sad and hurt. What additional feelings came up?" If the patient is still unable to get in touch with his anger, the therapist might ask, "What do you imagine someone else might have felt in that situation?"

The case that follows illustrates successful use of this technique.

This approach was most useful with a patient who was having tremendous difficulty getting in touch with his rage at finding his wife in their bed with another man — insisting for nearly 30 minutes that all he felt was "upset and hurt." When finally asked how he thought another man might feel had he just walked into his bedroom and found his bed occupied by another man, he responded, "People kill for that. You read about it in the newspapers all the time!" To this the leader responded, "So others might be angry enough to kill in that situation. Perhaps you feel that if you were to let yourself get in touch with your feelings you would be totally out of control."

Another strategy for dealing with the patient who is out of touch with feelings of rage is for the therapist to play back the "expectable" feelings, but with reduced intensity. For example:

A patient who was repeatedly being imposed upon by his "always sweet" mother responded with passive aggression, while consistently disowning any conscious anger at her. When asked by the therapist, "Did you ever feel like telling mother off when these things happened?", the patient responded, "Oh no! My mother is so sweet and good, I'm sure that she has only my best interest at heart!" The therapist might help the patient to acknowledge and eventually to integrate his unacceptable feelings of rage by playing back the feelings in reduced intensity and in a manner that conveys that the feelings are understandable (and perhaps even "natural") under the circumstances. For example, the therapist might respond, "I can imagine that your mother's 'good intentions' might make it more difficult to say something to her if you do feel a little disappointed and irritated when she makes so many requests."

Slips of the tongue may also express hidden and disavowed feelings and wishes. Again, the therapist can help the patient to integrate these unacceptable thoughts and wishes by making them understandable, and thus more acceptable. For example:

A patient, after accidentally using the therapist's name in place of his wife's when stating his wishes to be alone with her for the weekend, attempted to recover ground by stating to the therapist, "I don't think I really wanted to be alone with you." To this, the therapist might say, "That was probably not a prominent thought. However, patients do often have thoughts about their therapists outside the hour, and perhaps you've also been aware of these." If further "normalization" around wishes and fantasies about the therapist is indicated, the therapist might address further comments to group members more generally. Thus, she might say, "My guess is that most everyone in this group at one time or another has had thoughts about me outside of the hour — what I might be like when I'm not here, how I spend my time, and many other kinds of thoughts and fantasies as well."

Sometimes when fantasies initially come up about either the leader or other group members, they are presented in a manner that is colorless and vague. To encourage their greater development and exploration, I sometimes find it helpful to ask if the patient is "editing." And I might inquire what the group member imagines might happen if he weren't quite so careful with his words. Generally in the exploration of concerns about what would happen if words were not being so carefully chosen, the underlying issues that are being defended against are gradually discussed.

Supporting Group Members' Strengths Before Asking Difficult Questions

Just as it is often helpful to use techniques to make difficult interpretations more palatable, there will be times when it will be useful to verbally reinforce the therapeutic alliance before asking difficult questions of the patient. A useful strategy is for the leader to precede what might otherwise have appeared to be an awkward or difficult question by noting, first, the strengths of an individual member (to whom the question is addressed) or of the group-as-a whole (if the question is directed to the group). For example, a new group has several members who are complaining about the therapist's role, and asking, "What is the leader's job, anyway? What do you do? What will you be giving us?" Rather than simply exploring such inquiries, group leaders might precede their own questions with comments such as the following: "You seem to be a thoughtful group — and clearly you have been doing some thinking about some of these things. What have you *observed* so far about the way we work?" To patients' replies, "You practically never answer direct questions — you don't seem to do much more than direct traffic in here; in fact, you seem to want us to do most of the work," leaders might respond, "What thoughts do you have about why we might choose to behave in this way?" or, "You have observed that we mostly reflect back what group members put out, and explore questions rather than answering them directly. Why might a leader choose to do this?"

Often in the process of exploring and observing the leader's behavior and formulating ideas about why leaders might deliberately choose the strategies that they are using, the group settles its initial discomfort. Sometimes, however, the group continues to press, and worries continue about whether group members will get what they came for and whether the leaders will "put out" enough. When this occurs, it may be helpful for the leaders to remind patients about their discussions in the pregroup interview about how a therapy group works and, in particular, about the role of the leaders. They might then point out, however, that since group members' dissatisfaction and worries persist about whether their needs will be met — despite their understanding of the initial ground rules — these issues probably reflect old concerns and fears about whether their needs will be adequately attended to. The group should be assured that these are important issues from the past, which the group will be dealing with.

Cutting into Boredom

Often the therapist (and group) may feel mesmerized, stuck, and bored. Headway in cutting through the boredom can often be made by taking the following steps: (1) making observations (or asking patients to do so) about what has been transpiring; (2) exploring *feelings* about the observations; and (3) connecting the feelings and observations to present and past group process. Thus, when the group seems stuck, even if the leader herself is confused about what is going on, I have found it useful to begin by asking for group members' observations. I might say, for example, "We're halfway through the meeting at this point; where have we been so far?" or, "What observations have people made about what we've been doing in here for the past 20 minutes?" I might then follow this with a question about how people feel about what we have been doing. Even when the group begins by defending (usually a bit lamely) what has been going on as "just fine," exploration of group members' feelings often helps to give the group leaders a clue as to what is happening.

The third step involves a hypothesis or interpretation that the leader puts out that may help the group to better understand what is happening. But even if the leader has no idea about what is going on and is not in a position yet to make any kind of formulation, she may enlist the group in solving the mystery. For example, the leader might say, "Though it seems like the group has enjoyed having a chance to 'catch up' and to find out more about what's been going on for various members in their home lives, it's unusual for this group to spend so much time focused outside the group. How might the amount of time we have spent on this be related to what went on *inside* the group during our last session?" I find that even when I have no recollection of what went on during the prior group that might have caused the current resistance, the group members inevitably provide the missing link. They respond with something like, "Oh, do you mean the stuff about how we feel about the therapist?" or, "You mean the fight that Bob and Jenny were having?" Once the group is engaged in this process, it is dislodged from the stuck position and is able, once again, to move forward.

So far we have been talking about dealing with a stuck *group*. Sometimes, however, the problem resides — at least for the moment — primarily in a given patient who seems to be lulling the group to sleep with extensive details of outside-of-group events which no one (including the speaker) seems very connected to. I try to begin an intervention with such a patient by making the optimistic assumption that the patient is trying to connect, to be understood, and to share something of himself. There is probably always *some* truth to this assumption, although what we often experience is more the defense against the wish for closeness and sharing than the wish itself. The notion of giving support and empathy before making a potentially painful intervention has been addressed by Shay (1988) "empathize before you criticize" (p. 35); Stanton and Todd (1982), "ascribing noble intentions" (p. 125); and Cooper (1987), who advises, when confrontation is necessary, that the therapist use "his understanding of the patient's psychodynamics to intervene in a manner that will not injure the patient or raise his defensiveness too much" (p. 62). (This theme has also been discussed in earlier sections of this text — for example, in the sections "Making Interpretations More Palatable" and "Supporting Strengths before Asking Difficult Questions.")

The patient who is difficult to interrupt can often be stopped with a comment such as the following: "It is clear that there is a lot going on that you want the group to know about." This part of the statement allies with whatever good intentions there may be to communicate or to "be known." Then I might say, "But I wonder if I could stop you for just a minute to find out what's been going on in others as you've been talking." This gives the group members a chance either to comment on what the patient has been talking about, or to share similar or parallel experiences. It may also give them a chance, as is frequently the case, to make a comment indicating that they have long ago "tuned out." A patient may say for example, "I don't know, I was just in my own thoughts somewhere." I might then say, "Any thoughts about what might be going on that kept you from being tuned in while John was talking?" This often opens the way for the group members to express their reactions to the speaker and to provide useful (and often modifying) feedback.

The group can also be lulled to sleep by a patient who decides to bring in a written document that he has prepared during the week, or a document that has been written by someone else that the patient wishes to share. Generally, the patient's wish to read the material — sometimes in its entirety — reflects considerable anxiety and a need to contain his feelings by sharing the material in a controlled way. When the patient initially asks if he may read the material, it is generally helpful to ask the patient if he could first try to summarize it for the group. (This suggests the possibility that reading it might still be an option after the summary has taken place. However, in my experience, after a summary has been given it is usually not necessary.) Occasionally, when a patient is terribly anxious, he may feel compelled to proceed with the entire reading, without a summary. In the rare instances in which this has occurred in our groups, the prepared text has generally been read in an affectless fashion, filled with obsessional detail that the patient used to help bind his feelings. As such it was also generally very difficult to tune in to. To refocus the group after this kind of presentation, the leader might comment, "It is clear that there are many important thoughts and feelings expressed in your notes. Can you give us a little more of a sense of what, *in particular*, you are hoping the group will respond to." This helps the patient to focus and provides a guide to the group (and the leader) about where to go with the flood of material that the patient has produced.

At times, leaders may attempt to intervene in these kinds of difficult situations by "hitting the defense over the head" — for example, by pointing out to the patient that "he is flooding the group with details" or that he is "focused on things outside of the group." Although this may succeed in cutting off a patient at that particular moment, I generally find this approach relatively ineffectual in the long run and prefer a comment that conveys an optimism that group members (including this particularly difficult one) are *trying* to connect. Thus, the message to the patient is, "What are you *hoping* that the group will understand about you from what you are sharing?"

It should be noted that stopping patients, or cutting them off, is often difficult for the therapist even when (or perhaps especially when) he has grown bored. However, nowhere in the therapists' Hippocratic oath is it written that we are duty bound to be bored. In fact, generally we do the group (as well as ourselves) a disservice by remaining so. Thus, when the therapist recognizes that he is having these kinds of feelings he should do something to deal with them. Occasionally the simple decision to "tune in better" may do, or an examination (briefly in the group and perhaps more extensively afterwards) of the therapist's own defensive operations that may be causing him to tune out at the moment.

In my own experience I generally find that a broad, somewhat open-ended process question to the group not only helps to wake me up, but also is useful in dislodging the group from its "stuck" position. For example, when two members have been engaged in a lengthy dialogue that seems to have excluded other members, as well as the therapist, the therapist might ask the group, "How has what has been going on between Martha and Jim been helpful?" Perhaps I have been missing something, and the encounter really is meaningful to the group in some way that I have not recognized. On the other hand, if group members say, "Actually, it hasn't been terribly useful," I might inquire about people's thoughts about their letting it continue. Alternatively, I might direct the question specifically to the two people who are exclusively engaged with one another by asking, "What do you hope to have happen from the process that you have been engaged in for the past few minutes?" As is often true of process comments to the group, the therapist does not have to have an answer in mind when asking the group to reflect upon what is going on. Her only intention need be to "nudge" the group a bit to move it out of its current stuck position.

Dealing with a Member Who Is Invested in Not Getting Better

Occasionally, we encounter a group member who seems to be invested in staying permanently stuck. His life is wretched and miserable, relationships fail, job performance is poor, and in the group itself he seems to assume a depressed, wretched, unmovable position. No input from fellow group members or the leaders is perceived to be useful by such a patient, and the continued wretched nature of his life seems to serve as a "living testimonial" to the leader's, the group's, and his parents' "failure." Sometimes, such patients are powerfully motivated by a wish to retaliate — to punish or "get even" with those who are seen as providing too little (initially the parents, now the group and the leaders). It is as if such patients, by their very existence, testify to the failures of those who should have cared but were inadequate. The wish to punish by one's abject misery (rarely conscious) is often so powerful that actions congruent with this position continue to recur, at great cost to the patient. Such patients cling to their wretchedness, not because they are "masochistic," not because they truly wish to suffer, but, rather, because of a powerful wish to punish others. Some patients often say directly to their therapists, "No therapist has ever helped me yet, and I doubt that any will be able to," or, "Others have been useless to me, and I doubt that you will be any better."

Epstein (1979) discusses his experience with patients stuck in this kind of regressive position, indicating,

> The persecuted child seeks vengeance and retaliates by frustrating the parent, going on strike for protracted periods of time, becoming passive, helpless, too infirm to perform — thereby inducing further attacks from the frustrated parent. (p. 257)

He then describes a patient engaged in self-destructive behavior, which the therapist interpreted as "his way of equalizing things," suggesting to the patient that "if he got hurt or killed it would be a sad commentary on my (therapist's) analytic competence" (p. 267). In a similar vein, Searles (1979) points out that the therapist engaged in such a struggle loses sight of

> . . . how much sadistic gratification the patient is deriving from his therapist's anguished, tormented, futile dedication. He does not realize . . . (as) one chronically schizophrenic man confide(d) to his therapist, "The pleasure I get in torturing you is the main reason I go on staying in this hospital."
>
> Further, the dedicated therapist does not see how much ambivalence the patient has about change, even change for the "better." He does not see that the patient has reached his present equilibrium only after years of thought and effort and the exercise of the best judgement of which he is capable. (p. 74)

Clearly, such patients cannot be helped by group leaders (or the group) struggling with them to get better. In fact, the harder the group tries, the greater their defeat (and in a way, the greater the patient's "victory"). Rather than struggling with such a patient to convince him to get better or to suggest alternative options or to give advice (as group members are often inclined to do), it may be helpful for group leaders to gently suggest the possibility of this underlying dynamic. Leaders may say something such as, "It is clear, John, that you feel wretched and depressed most of the time. It is also clear that there is some part of you that wishes that this were not so. But since your wretchedness continues, despite the input of a myriad of therapists and repeated therapeutic encounters of different kinds, I wonder if there is some other part of you that might stand to gain by remaining stuck as you are. Perhaps there is some other part of you that feels that you might be losing out on some kind of moral victory were you to allow yourself to make even a little bit of progress." Alternatively, the therapist might share his speculation about a possible retaliative motive that might be operating with a comment such as, "I knew a patient who went to incredible self-destructive lengths to keep himself in his wretched and unbearable situation as a way of giving a message to his parents. It was almost as if his repeated failure was designed to punish them for failing him so miserably when he needed them as a child. I wonder if anything like that might be operating for you?"

When such patients appear to be making progress in their lives — actually showing signs of improved relationships with others and better job performance, their self-presentation with the group often remains as wretched, despairing, and hopeless as ever. When this occurs, the therapist might comment, "Alongside of many markers that might lead you (and perhaps myself and the group) to infer that you might be getting a little better, you seem to have a powerful wish to assure us that you are no better off, and perhaps even getting worse. How might we understand this?"

An example of this dynamic recently came to my attention.

A young woman in a group that I supervise had had a series of therapeutic failures, accompanied by two prior successes, in getting her therapists (who also felt that they had failed) to let her pile up extensive debts. (One of the therapists, upon her termination, seemingly acknowledged his own failure by tearing up, in her presence, her page in his billing ledger.) Now, with her group therapist, she was again complaining about his ineptitude and the enormous cost of the sessions. (Though she was paying less than half of the therapist's usual fee, even this was perceived to be too costly given her "negligible progress.") This patient had managed not only to defeat a host of therapists by her lack of progress (punctuated by complaints of getting worse), but had further defeated two of them by defaulting on large sums of money, and was currently hoping to again set up a therapy situation in which her financial cost would be negligible. Her group therapist appropriately handled this complicated situation by suggesting to the patient that she had been in a series of therapy experiences in which she expected the therapist to bear most of the cost, while she invested little. The therapist pointed out that, in fact, such therapies were probably not worth paying for and if she did want to make headway in therapy she (as well as the therapist) would have to invest. It would be her choice as to whether she wanted to continue the pattern of the past or really get down to work in the therapy — but the latter would require making a reasonable investment.

Turning a "Bad" Group Around

There will be times in the course of any group when it feels temporarily stuck. There is another kind of impasse, however, that is far more difficult to deal with. This occurs in the group that has developed a "lethal culture" in which existing members terminate prematurely and new members are seemingly "gobbled up." For example:

> One group went through an eight-month period with high attrition of old members and concerns that the group was "dying," combined with an unwarm and unreceptive response when new members were added. New members, even those who were carefully picked for this particular group for their heartiness and for the sense of hope and enthusiasm they might infuse into the group, generally lasted only a few sessions. Although the group leaders continued to invest in the group, it was "a losing battle." The group leader who had preceded the current co-leader team had been a cold, unresponsive therapist who projected her own "uncaring" feelings onto the group. During one supervision, in fact, she commented, "The trouble with this group is that members just don't care at all about each other." Although this group leader eventually left the group, the uncaring culture seemed to continue.
>
> Ultimately, a decision was made to "reconstitute the group." That is, instead of continuing to refer new members, either individually or in combination (either way ultimately to fail), the group leaders told the members that the group, as it now existed, was too small to continue and that it had been a difficult group for new members to settle into. They indicated that they would be forming a new group on the same night, but a half hour later, and that the three existing members would all be invited to join. In the spirit of the new, reconstituted group, group leaders then had pregroup interviews again with the three existing members, as well as with the new members that they were bringing in, and set a target date one month later for beginning the "new group." Only in this way was the "lethal culture," which had been transmitted through several generations of the group, finally undermined.

Getting the Group to Ally with the Therapist's Integrity

Often, when a group is struggling with its leader by objecting to particular leader behavior that seems "harsh," it may be helpful to enlist the group's observing ego around allying with the therapist's integrity. For example:

A patient who was making serious suicide threats was hospitalized involuntarily by her group leader a few hours after the group session ended. When the patient came to the next session she was enraged about the therapist's "precipitous action" and disregard for her clearly stated wishes not to be hospitalized. The group rallied to support the "incarcerated" patient and to criticize the leader's hastiness and unfairness. The leader, instead of behaving defensively, or telling the group why she had done what she did, asked the following: "As a mental health professional charged with the task of seeing to it that her patients do not seriously harm themselves or others, how might a leader reasonably behave?" She then went on to ask, "What course of action would one reasonably expect of a therapist under these circumstances?" and, "How would group members have felt, knowing that I, as the group leader, seriously concerned about whether Pam might be a danger to herself or to her kids, did nothing to protect her?"

Another example of enlisting group support for the therapist's integrity occurred in a situation in which a group member asked the group leaders to "bend the truth slightly" in order to help him collect insurance payments. More specifically:

The patient, who had considerable insurance benefits, had neglected to submit his forms for an entire year, two years earlier. The deadline for filing these forms had now passed. However, the patient had learned from the insurance company that a waiver would be possible were he able to document that his psychopathology had interfered with his ability to organize himself adequately to get the necessary paper work in. Although the request to the group leaders did not, in fact, seem terribly unreasonable (this patient had, in fact, been depressed throughout that period), the wording of his initial request tipped the leaders off that they might do well to explore the matter more fully. More specifically, the patient prefaced his request with the comment, "I have a slightly 'uncouth' request to make of the leaders." When they asked how he would feel if the letter were not forthcoming, he responded that he would be quite disappointed, as this would cost him roughly $1500. To further inquiries about how he would feel about his leaders doing something that he considered "uncouth," he responded that he had always been impressed with their integrity and that maybe he needed to think a bit more about how he would feel if he got them *to do something that "wasn't quite right." He returned the next week to inform the group, that in fact, he could very well have filled out the forms, and that he preferred not to ask the leaders to do something which he felt would impugn their integrity.*

Protecting Patients Who Fear Their Feelings Will Be Too Intense (Sane Pain Control Strategy)

Part of our task as group therapists is to help our patients expand their ability to explore important and, often, painful experiences. For the patient who fears that the pain involved in getting close to feelings may be too intense or too overwhelming, it is helpful if she and the therapist can come up with a mechanism that will enable the patient to signal that she is in pain before the pain gets to be too great. An analogy that I have found helpful comes from my dentist's "sane pain control strategy." He asks his patients to raise their index finger as soon as the drilling begins to hurt. When he gets the signal, he stops temporarily, inquires about the pain, asks what has just changed, and asks the patient to suggest how she would like to "cool things down" at that point (e.g., a swig of water, some cool air, just relaxing for a moment, etc.). The most important aspect of this procedure is that the dentist conveys to his patient that she will have some *control* over the amount of pain that will be experienced by being able to signal when she feels it is getting to be too great (or if she even *fears* that it is beginning to get too intense). The dentist's plan, of course, is not to *stop* the process, since ultimately his task is to complete the job; rather, his task is to try to find a way of proceeding in greater comfort.

Similarly, in the therapy situation, the idea is not to stop when overwhelmed with pain or afraid of potential future pain, but to take a *temporary* break in order to take stock of the situation and to talk about what will be needed to cool things off — in order, ultimately, to proceed. Sometimes it may be useful to convey this analogy directly to the patient, before asking her to collaborate with the group in designating the signal that she will use to "cool things off." Other group members may also be useful, as collaborators in reading the "pain signals," and in providing the agreed upon "cooling down" procedures (such as temporarily refocusing the discussion — to return to the difficult material later in the session; or focusing, instead, on related issues that others in the group may experience).

Dealing with Resistance When It Comes Packaged as "Reality"

Frequently, reality in the patient's (or our own) life can serve to aid and abet resistance. Thus, when a patient presents an understandable "explanation" for being late or for missing a session, it is helpful for the therapist to keep in mind that life is full of events that provide good excuses for avoiding things. These events are real (bad weather, car troubles, not feeling well.) However, many of these "excuses of everyday life" are such that one might still be in a position to attend the session, and to arrive on time, were one sufficiently motivated to do so. The obvious test of this, of course, is that often the very patient who stays away because she is "not feeling well" may have come to group "under the weather" in the past. Or, the patient who is "detained at work" has on other occasions been able to set clear limits with his boss — indicating that he has a prior commitment. Thus, the therapist should keep an open mind to exploring possible resistance, even when the explanation of absence or late arrival or other forms of avoidance (e.g., sleepiness in group, minimal participation, etc.) seems quite plausible. For example:

> Recently, in a group that typically begins and ends on time, six out of seven patients arrived late. All offered "weather" as the explanation. Indeed, the roads were a bit more slippery that night, due to heavy rains. But this group had had an excellent track record even during periods of heavy snow. The group leader, remembering that the previous session had been a difficult one and suspecting that resistance might also be a factor, said, "The roads are a bit more slippery tonight than usual. Yet people in here have had a track record of timely attendance even on some of the worse nights in the history of Boston. Could there be other factors, relating to what happened last week in the group, that made it even harder for people to get here on time tonight?" The leader, here, was thus

supporting the reality but, in addition, wondering whether more might be going on as well.

In one of my own groups a member sat through much of one session looking tired, sleepy, and bored. I commented to him, "You seem to be less with us tonight than usual." The patient responded, "I'm just exhausted — had a really hard day at work," and provided some details to substantiate this. I responded, "It sounds like it has been a rough day, but I wonder if, in addition, it might be harder to stay awake in here because of what happened in here during the last session." In this instance I might alternatively have chosen to link my exploration of possible resistance to events in the group in the preceding half hour — or if I thought there might be more payoff to choosing a longer time frame, I might have picked "the past few weeks." What is important here is that the therapist first *validate* the reality and then add that, in addition to the reality, it might be even harder to come on time, stay awake, etc., due to group issues.

From our own personal experience all of us know this phenomenon well. An important meeting is planned that we are not particularly interested in going to and we wake up suddenly with a sore throat. We now have a reasonable excuse for not attending — but one which probably would not have been invoked had the event been one we were really interested in participating in.

Co-Therapy Strategies

Co-therapy can be useful, not only in helping leaders keep track of the many complicated dynamics in these groups, but also for role-modeling healthy dyadic communication.* Although I particularly like the use of a male-female co-therapy team, because this heightens the family transference, same sex co-therapists can also be effective in modeling adaptive communication — including effective ways in which people can clarify and "check in" with one another, and adaptive ways of disagreeing.

---

*Many of the advantages of co-therapy and the specific technique discussed in this section and the next have also been discussed with regard to the group treatment of alcoholic couples (Vannicelli, 1987).

To model mechanisms for clarifying communication, it is often helpful if the co-leaders make a somewhat self-conscious effort to "pair" in constructive ways in the group. For example, it may be helpful for a co-therapist to reiterate what the other leader has just said (especially if the message has been a bit confusing) by asking, "Were you saying . . .?" and rephrasing the communication. Alternatively, the co-leaders may discuss a possible decision openly with one another in front of the group. For example, one leader may say, "I was thinking that one thing we might do is suggest to Mr. X that he take a leave of absence from the group until he can arrange his work schedule to make more regular attendance at the group possible. What do you think?" The co-therapist might then respond, "Yes, I think that's a good idea, but it also occurred to me that we might give Mr. X another week to come back to hear the group's input before we implement that decision." The two co-leaders might then talk about the pros and cons with one another in front of the group, while also asking for the group's input.

Modeling effective *disagreement* can also be very useful — the co-leaders actively disagreeing with one another, either about an interpretation or about the best next strategy. For example, one leader might say to the other, "You were suggesting that Mr. X might take a leave of absence. I have a different idea that we might consider." Or, "Yes, I can see your thinking there, but I had a very different thought." It is most helpful if these kinds of exchanges communicate that each leader has heard the message of the other, has taken it quite seriously, but may see things from a different vantage point. If the leaders model respect for one another and genuine processing of each other's messages, they are in a particularly good position to also model for the group the ways in which people can disagree without being destructive.

Clarifying the Mechanisms of Miscommunication

One of the most important leader tasks is to help clarify messages (and miscommunications) as well as partial communications that get transmitted. One technique that I have found useful is to call attention to the miscommunication by first asking the person to whom the message has been addressed how he understood what was being communicated. Often this will disclose to the speaker that his intention has been misunderstood. Next, I turn to the person who has been communicating and ask what, in fact, he *meant* to say. Pointing out the discrepancies between what has been *said* and what has been *heard* can be very useful in helping members understand how their communications can get scrambled. Other group members may also provide helpful input to the speaker about aspects of the communication that may have been confusing (e.g., additional messages that may have been communicated by tone of voice, as well as possible distortions on the part of the listener.)

Tips on Termination

An area of frequent concern among therapists, in both group and individual therapy, is how actively to intervene when a patient raises the issue of termination before the therapist believes he is ready to leave. Countertransference (as well as transference) issues are often important to consider, and it is useful for the therapist to explore her own feelings about the patient, the work that remains to be done, and her feelings about saying good-bye to this particular patient. Often, patients who are in the height of negative transference (and stirring up equally negative countertransference feelings in the therapist) are all too willingly let go by a frustrated therapist. Conversely, therapists may feel especially attached to, or identified with, some of their patients. With these patients there is often a feeling that "things are still not yet totally complete — work remains to be done." That is, there is a wish for perfect closure. Often, as well, the therapist identifies with the patient's separation issues, and these get acted out in the therapist's reluctance to hear that the patient may be ready to leave.

One way of exploring the issue, which allows the the therapist to collect more information about the patient's readiness or nonreadiness to leave, is for the therapist to ask the patient the following questions: (1) "What is it that you first came to work on?" and (2) "Where do things now stand with that?"

If the patient feels that there is still more to be done but that he "can't get at it anymore," the therapist might ask, "What makes you feel there is still more to do? What are the indicators, in terms of the experiences that come up for you, that suggest that this is still a problem?" If the patient cannot produce much material, it may be that, indeed, at this point in the work the territory has been sufficiently covered. Sometimes, because of the therapist's own feelings about the termination or her own wishes for a more "perfect product," she may have difficulty accepting the idea of a termination.

When my patients begin to consider termination (particularly, premature termination), I often find it useful to discuss with them the various ways that people leave a therapy group. I tell them that there are three points at which people generally think about leaving therapy, and that each is associated with different kinds of goal resolutions, different feelings about leaving, and different ways of handling the termination. After reviewing these three routes of termination (generally in considerably fewer words than the descriptions I have outlined below), I ask the potential terminator to classify himself by indicating which of these categories he thinks his proposed termination most closely matches. In most instances I find that patients are reasonably accurate in placing themselves, or at worst, put themselves between two categories (with one of the categories being the one I would also see as the most likely). This provides a forum for discussing with the patient where he is in his therapy.

The three categories of termination are as follows:

1. *Completers*: Completers have essentially finished the work that they came in for and are sufficiently educated regarding the benefits of group work that they understand, also, the impact of doing the last phase of work, saying good-bye. They also understand that saying good-bye is a process — something that we all need to learn how to do better — and that the therapy group offers a unique opportunity to learn how to do this. These patients are able to review their goals and gains in therapy as well as reflect upon their losses, as they think about giving up the group and how it will feel, ultimately, to be gone.

2. *Plateauers*: These patients have done some of the work that they came in for but have a sense that they are not really finished. Rather, for the time being, they are "stuck." Plateauers

have no clear sense of what more can be accomplished at the present time. (Often these patients return to treatment at a later point.) These patients are able to do some of the work of saying good-bye, although usually in a more abbreviated way than completers. The good-byes serve as the last focused project that the patient can gain from working on.

3. *Fleers*: (This group may also be referred to as "Flyers") These patients experience a pressing need to "get out." In fact the pressure to leave is often the telling signal of the fleer. Such patients cannot take the time to terminate, but, rather, feel tremendous pressure to leave in haste. Generally patients in this category are avoiding something in the group, or in themselves, that they feel uncomfortable about and from which they wish to flee as rapidly as possible.

Another route for dealing with a patient who is facing the possibility of termination is to inquire what the patient believes he might work on if he remained in the group. Sometimes, this is a way of getting at what the patient might be avoiding or taking flight from. Sometimes, it may simply confirm that the patient does not feel in sufficient pain at the moment to warrant further continuation in therapy, or that perhaps the work is, in fact, essentially done.

Ending the Session

Termination of a different sort, a "mini-termination," occurs at the end of each session. Such endings can also cause difficulty for the therapist who may feel uncomfortable ending the group on time, particularly if a member of the group has raised an important topic close to the end of the session, or if the group as a whole is intensely engaged in affectively loaded material. "Dropping a bomb" at the end of a session, as Kanfer and Schefft (1988) point out, may be motivated by a variety of factors including the patient's ambivalence about getting into potentially conflictual material or his wish for reassurance of the leader's (or group's) interest, which he hopes to see demonstrated by their willingness to prolong the therapy session. However, "unless there is clear and immediate threat to the welfare of the client or other persons, discussion of the issue should be delayed until the following session" (p. 346). Consistently ending the session on time — a clear behavioral statement regarding the ground rules and boundaries of the group — is the best mechanism, in the long run, for decreasing the likelihood of future "hit and run" interactions. As Kanfer and Schefft point out, "The message should be conveyed that it is the client's responsibility to initiate the discussion of important topics *within* the allotted time for therapy" (p. 346).

Therapeutic interventions that may be useful in lessening the patient's feeling of being "cut off" might include the following: As soon as the patient brings up the difficult material, and the leader is aware that very little time remains, he might say something like, "The issue that you are raising sounds like a very important one for you. It's too bad that we have so little time left tonight to talk about it, but hopefully we will have a chance to explore it more fully in our next session." In this way the leader has set the stage, even before the last seconds of the group, to indicate that the time boundaries of the group will be maintained. Even so, the last seconds of the group may feel very intense either because a given individual is in the middle of a very difficult issue or the group, as a whole, is engaged in very intense work. In this instance the "blow" of ending can be softened to some extent by a comment such as, "This is a hard place to stop, but our time is up. Hopefully we will be able to discuss this more next session."

Thoughts on Names and Other "Distancing" Issues

What patients and group leaders call one another (first name or last) is handled in a variety of ways by different therapists. Many models are commonly used: (1) both use last names; (2) both use first names; (3) a casual mix of these with no fixed policy and differing from one patient to the next; and (4) the therapist is called by her last name, but addresses patients by their first names. (The only combination that I have not encountered is one where the patients address the group therapist by her first name and she uses last names to address group members.) While the success or failure of a group will obviously not hinge on matters of nomenclature, my own strong preference is for a symmetrical relationship in which patient and therapist are both either on a first name or last name basis. The not so uncommon model where the therapist is addressed by last name (Dr. so-and-so) and patients by first names (Martha, Jenny, Susie) can potentially infantilize the patient, which I think is particularly unfortunate and to be avoided in ACOA groups. I am also generally less enthused about a "whatever name anyone wishes to use is fine" model in a group context because it makes it harder to examine shifts that occur, and some interesting pieces of process can potentially be lost.

I would like to describe a naming model that I have found to be particularly productive during the initial phases of ACOA groups — even though this is a model that many therapists may not initially feel comfortable with — that is, the use of last name by both therapist and patient. When we are beginning the introductory groups in our clinic, we tell group members, as we do the initial introductions, that the policy in our clinic is for patients to address leaders by last name and for leaders to "give equal respect" by addressing group members in the same way.

The group's response to this policy, generally, is to unify and object. Thus, early on, members are establishing a we/they dichotomy in the group (i.e., members separate and distinct from leaders). They usually agree that regardless of what we, the leaders, will call them, they will call one another by first name. (If there is any question about this, we also let them know that they are free to call one another whatever they choose.) The use of first names among members, but last between members and leaders, sets a kind of boundary or differentiation between members and leaders. We have found that this not only reflects a certain reality about the way the group functions (after all, the leader's role is quite different, in many ways, from the members') but also binds the members more closely to one another. This starting point also sets the distinction, from the outset, between the therapy group and the Al-Anon or ACOA groups that many of the patients belong to, where all participants are on first name basis. This distinction, in the long run, will also be useful since, indeed, a therapy group is quite different from an Al-Anon group, where there are no leaders and where the process itself is quite different.

The initial protest — with the group joined against the leader — also serves to test the leader's resilience. Group members have an opportunity to openly confront the leaders, to state objections, and to learn that the leaders can tolerate disagreement from members. The group is calmed by the leader's comfort in handling members' objections, and members are assured that they do not have to be on "good" behavior in order for the group to proceed.

Finally, and perhaps of most interest, this model brings to focus, within the first few minutes of the group, a key issue that the group will be struggling with — namely, intimacy and closeness. For many patients the immediate response is to project onto the leaders a wish for distance. That is, that "the leaders are setting it up so that it will not be intimate in here." The members thus project their own problems with intimacy onto the leaders. When this initially comes up, it is helpful if leaders can underscore the importance of this initial issue by saying something like, "You have raised an important issue that I think many of you bring to this group about how close you will be able to get to others. That you have concerns about how close people in here will be able to get to one another is natural and something that we will be working on and coming to better understand as our work in here proceeds."

Some readers' reaction to the leaders' use of last names may be that, indeed, the leaders are setting up distance, and that it is not a "projection of the patients" at all — but rather, that the patients are realistically responding to the actual data at hand. I think it is important, however, to consider that even when the "objective data" would seem to support the patients' views, what patients make of the data may still be important in helping us to understand their issues. It is true that the leaders have chosen to use last names. They have not, however, done so in *order* to create distance or because they have problems with intimacy. That the members may infer these motives is, in all likelihood, a reflection of issues that are important to the members, themselves, and are being projected onto the therapist.

Let me share another example that I think will help illuminate this.

> For some time in the office where I saw my individual clients my chair was situated, relative to the three available client chairs, in such a way that a client could choose to sit on the other side of my desk at some distance, at the other side of my desk more directly across from me, or directly across from me with no desk in between.

A young male patient whom I had been seeing for several weeks began to complain about how "cold and distant" I was. He cited the fact that I asked for him by last name when I had called him at work, and that I kept a huge distance between us with my large desk. (It should be noted that he had chosen the seat, not only on the other side of the desk, but also at the greatest distance from me — the only patient I have ever treated who chose that seat.) When I asked how it was that he had chosen that particular chair, he looked around, as if for the first time, and stated, "Well you never had that other chair (pointing to the one closest to me that would have left no desk between us) until today!" I indicated that, in fact, that chair had been there for several years and wondered what thoughts he had about not having noticed it before. He laughed, a little self-consciously, and said, "Funny that I didn't notice it. Maybe it's I who wants the distance." The next week he came in, briefly tried out the closer seat, shifted around in it for a few minutes, and then indicated that it was "not nearly as comfortable as the other chair" (which was identical) and returned to his "more comfortable place."

It is clear in this instance that the patient *was* responding to some real data. I *had* used his last name when I called him at work, and there *was* a large desk between us. However, neither of these "facts" changed the important issue — namely, that the patient's projections about my "coldness and distance" were important indicators of his own issues.

It is also important to note that even when a patient has *accurately* identified one of the therapist's issues (perhaps I am one of the more formal, "distant" therapists) — that is, even when the patient's perception appears to be 'factual'— his reactions are still important indicators of his own issues. As Searles (1979) points out, it is often "those real increments of the analyst's personality functioning which serve, for the patient, as the nuclei of external reality that evokes his transference reactions" (p. 393). Thus, the therapist's interest in exploring the patient's fantasies about him should not in any way be inhibited by the therapist's own appraisal of the "accuracy" of the patient's perception.

What's in a Name: A Clinical Example

In the preceding discussion the issue of names was examined from the standpoint of the distancing issues that may be raised for the patient. Attention to names can be equally important in understanding other aspects of the patient's dynamics, as illustrated in the following case example.

> Ms. Abel, a young woman in her mid 30s, presented for her pregroup interview with considerable depression and accompanying feelings of being "stuck" in nearly every area of her life. In the weeks prior to seeking treatment she had gotten in touch with a growing awareness that these "bad feelings" about herself related to a long standing sense of being devalued and unappreciated by her highly successful (and neglectful) mother, who had had little time or energy for mothering the patient and her twin brother. Despite the patient's continuous efforts to gain recognition from her mother, the brother was "from the start, the only one she ever noticed." Now, despite Ms. Abel's considerable personal and financial investment in her mother's multimillion-dollar fashion design company, a coalition was being formed by her mother and brother which appeared to be "squeezing her out" (an injustice aggravated by the patient's "day-in-day-out" devotion to the company during the past five years).
>
> At the second pregroup interview, the group leader addressed Ms. Abel in the waiting room by her last name. As they proceeded down the corridor to her office, the patient said, "Please call me Beth, I don't feel old enough yet to feel like a 'Ms.' When I'm in the office with my mother, every time someone says Ms. Abel to me, I look over my shoulder, thinking that they mean my mom." The leader then inquired, "Is there a part of you that feels that the status of 'Ms.' belongs only to your mother?" Ms. Abel responded, "I suppose so, but I'm also a pretty informal kind of gal." The group leader then asked, "How do you feel about your mom being called Ms. Abel?" The patient replied, "I feel that she deserves that kind of respect." At this point the leader asked how these "naming issues" might relate to feelings the patient had raised about her dwindling status in the company (and in the family). The patient responded, "Perhaps there is a connection; my brother also likes to be called 'Mr.' since he likes to see himself as the 'heir apparent.'" Ms. Abel then volunteered that not only were last names significant in her family but that nicknames, too, continued to reflect familial status. She continued to be called Bitsy and sometimes Bittybetz by her mother (to her chagrin even, occasionally, in front of clients.) In contrast, her brother, "the rising star," had long since abandoned his childhood name (Benji) and for many years had been referred to

only by his given name, Benjamin. The patient then indicated that additional "naming" problems had also emerged at work, where Ms. Abel found herself at odds as to what to call her mother — feeling "little girlish" saying "Mom" in front of clients, yet feeling equally uncomfortable referring to her mother by either her first name or her last.

When the therapist inquired whether in professional settings, outside of the family business, the patient had found similar difficulties, she responded, "Oh, not at all. In the two years that I worked for Smith Associates, I was always referred to as Ms. Abel. Smith Associates was a professional place in which all business was conducted on a last name basis, and it was clear that that was what was appropriate." At that point, the therapist explained that her preference professionally was to be referred to as Dr. Jones, and that she thought it appropriate to accord her group members equal respect by referring to them by last name, as well. She then added that she suspected that Ms. Abel would continue to have feelings about this in the group from time to time and that, hopefully, she would feel comfortable talking about them.

What this vignette demonstrates is that the naming issue reflected not a casual preference of a "laid back kind of gal," but, rather, the patient's unconscious wish to reestablish with the group leader the diminutive role that paralleled her conflict in her family of origin. The leader's message, instead, indicated that she would be regarding the patient as a respected adult.

Avoiding Nontherapeutic Encounters

Throughout this chapter the focus has been on things the therapist can *do* to further the work of the therapy. Much of the material has focused on delineating the role of the therapist, as well as the limits of the therapeutic relationship. However, because of powerful wishes "to help better," and "to do more," the therapist may at times feel pulled to do more than is, in fact, appropriate. And so, in closing this chapter a few words are in order about what *not* to do when patients tug for more.

The limits of the therapeutic relationship have been articulately discussed, with considerable overlap in points of view, by therapists from the cognitive behavioral tradition (Kanfer &

Schefft, 1988) as well as by those from the more traditional psychodynamic orientation (Cooper, 1988; Wood, 1987). Cooper discusses this from the standpoint of "therapeutic neutrality." He states,

> The neutral stance, combined with our constant efforts to remain empathically attuned, keeps us very involved with our patients, but as a psychotherapist rather than as a friend or parent or lover. . . . (As such,) over time patients come to appreciate that we are involved with them in a different enterprise from that to which they are accustomed, and that it is our interest in them and our respect for their autonomy which leads us to remain neutral. (p. 8)

Kanfer and Schefft (1988) similarly warn that the therapist needs to "guard against the expectation by the client that an intense emotional involvement will develop between them" — in particular, "the client's expectations of extending the relationship to one in which the therapist assumes the role of a parent or lover" (p. 103). These authors reinforce the boundaries of the therapy relationship and the limits on the therapist's behavior by clearly articulating the distinction between social and therapeutic interactions. More specifically they state,

> Warmth and acceptance are communicated by the therapist, but in her role as a professional whose genuine interest and concern are due chiefly to her desire to assist the client. The style and purpose of the interaction, the content of the conversation, and the structure of the relationship sharply differentiate social interactions from therapeutic interactions. (p. 297)

They then go on to point to a number of important distinctions between therapeutic and social interactions. First, the rules of "social politeness" do not apply in the usual sense. In fact, socially graceful statements are best kept to a minimum because "social politeness may increase the likelihood that the client will engage in conversation that is superficial and unrelated to the therapeutic task, following an automatic pattern determined by social etiquette" (p. 298). Second, social and therapeutic interactions differ in that social conversation is bidirectional. This is in contrast to therapeutic conversation which occurs in a dyadic relationship, but is unidirectional — that is, while the content reflects personal material from the patient, it "does not encompass material from the clinician's personal life" (p. 299). Third, therapeutic interactions are deliberate and purposeful — constantly being guided by the intended or anticipated consequence of any given intervention statement. This is very different from the spontaneous nature of social interactions, which put relatively few demands on either participant to be either deliberate or self-reflective. Kanfer and Schefft suggest that the deliberate style of the therapist is facilitated by avoiding "polite phrases, general opinions, or well-rehearsed automatic verbal sequences" (p. 300). For example, they suggest that it is not useful for a therapist to open the session with a question such as, "How are you?" (which pulls for an equally automatic response from the patient).

Wood (1987), addressing this same issue, also warns against the therapist's temptation to exceed the limits of the therapy relationship — particularly when feeling pressured by a patient's wish to be "held." Citing Guntrip (1969) and Winnicott (1954/ 1975), she indicates that "the therapist can adequately satisfy the longing that is being expressed by accepting and understanding the patient's need" (p. 85). That this issue is addressed so frequently in the literature is an indication, perhaps, of the tremendous pull that therapists often experience to extend the boundaries of the therapy relationship.

This chapter has examined a number of techniques that the group leader may use to further the work of the therapy. While such techniques may prove useful they are no substitute for adequate clinical training and preparation — the topic of the next chapter.

9

Preparation and Training
of the ACOA Group Therapist

with Dale Dillavou, Ph.D.

It is important for the ACOA group therapist to be knowledgeable not only about "adult-child issues" and group psychotherapy, but also about alcoholism itself. In this chapter we will outline the content areas necessary for the training and preparation of the ACOA group therapist, readings that will be helpful, and specialized group therapy training experiences that are available.

Information About Alcoholism

Knowledge about alcoholism is important: (1) for initial clinical assessment and appropriate triage (as described in Chapter 3) since many ACOAs will have problems with alcohol or will be worried about it, and/or will attach themselves to new intimates who have alcohol and drug problems; and (2) to avoid countertransference alliances around myths, misbeliefs, and negative stereotypes about alcoholics. The latter is important because many therapists (perhaps most) who are drawn to working with ACOAs will have had some personal experience with alcoholism (if not a relative, then somebody else with whom they were close in some way). These limited experiences may create a false sense of being knowledgeable, which, when combined with popular myths and misbeliefs about alcoholism, may serve to actually limit the therapist's effectiveness. Ironically, therapists who are themselves ACOAs and thus see themselves as having "lived through it" may be especially vulnerable to negative stereotyping of the alcoholic and to tunnel vision — both of which may impede the therapist's ability to help group members clarify some of their own faulty thinking. Thus, the therapist working with this population will benefit from knowing more about alcoholism — the progression of the illness, the many courses it may take, the many different ways it may become entwined in the family system, the ways the illness gets played out with significant others, and the treatment options.

Complexity of the Problem and Heterogeneity among Alcoholics

Alcoholism is a complex multifaceted problem. It has physiological, medical, psychological, behavioral, and interpersonal consequences. It affects many different kinds of people and in different ways. This tremendous diversity has given rise to the current view among alcohologists that it is more correct to refer to the "alcoholisms" rather than to alcoholism (Zucker, 1987), thereby capturing the tremendous variety in the people that become alcoholics (Pattison, 1985), the symptoms that they manifest (Cloninger, 1987; Pattison, 1985), the course of the illness (Cahalan, 1976; Clark & Cahalan, 1976), the course of recovery (Polich, Armor & Braiker, 1981), and in all likelihood, treatment options that are the most effective. There are few simple "generalizable facts" that are true of all alcoholics (despite the presence of a myriad of unsubstantiated but dearly held beliefs about alcoholism that pervade both the alcoholic and nonalcoholic communities). Understanding the presence or the severity of an alcohol problem requires more than simply knowing the frequency or quantity of usage, when and how it is used, or the physiological or psychological sequelae. What appears to be "alcoholism" under one cultural microscope may look different in a population with a different age group or different cultural background. Each of these factors is important and must be considered, but only in combination do we understand the full picture.

The important point here is the tremendous heterogeneity among alcoholics. Most alcoholics (some 93%) never enter treatment. Thus the clinician's view is hardly representative of the wider picture. As Steinglass, Bennett, Wolin, and Reiss (1987) point out, "most families with alcoholic members are relatively quiet types" — whose situation escapes detection, even by professionals (p. 6). The alcoholics that we see in treatment and those that are most visible in the community cannot be assumed to be representative of all, or even of most, alcoholics. Thus, each ACOA patient who enters treatment has his own window on alcoholism that may or may not overlap with his therapist's view.

Because alcoholism is so complex, and requires more than "common sense" understanding, we encourage the reader to expand his knowledge about it (we have provided an annotated bibliography to assist in selecting readings). Our hope is that the reader will develop a sense that much of what he already "knows" may not be entirely accurate. On a more optimistic note, the "truths" that we would pass on are the following: (1) People do not set out to become alcoholic. Alcoholism arises out of a complex interplay of predisposing genetic factors, psychological factors, and sociocultural factors. We are far from totally understanding the complex interplay. (2) Many alcoholics do get better (Saxe, Dougherty, Esty, & Fine, 1983; Vaillant et al., 1983), and when they do the quality of their lives and those of their families is often indistinguishable from that of those who are not alcoholic (Moos & Billings, 1982; Moos, Finney, & Chan, 1981; Moos & Moos, 1984). (3) Finally, treatment is available.

Treatment for Alcoholism

Most experts in the field of alcoholism agree that treatment begins with bringing the alcohol problem under control, though there may be some disagreement about whether this means behavioral control and management of the drinking (Pattison, 1985; Polich, Armor, & Braiker, 1980; Sobell & Sobell, 1973a,b, 1976) or total abstinence (Vaillant et al., 1983; Weisman & Robe, 1983; Zimberg, 1982). Treatment is generally thought to be indicated when alcohol use has significant negative consequences in any area of the patient's life (physical or psychological health, relationships, employment), yet the use of alcohol persists (Pattison, 1985). Increasingly, clinicians who treat the problem recognize that by the time treatment is indicated (1) the substance abuse has developed a life and a momentum of its own which needs to be treated in its own right (that is, that the alcohol problem will not go away by itself simply because the underlying, or accompanying, problems are being treated); and (2) halting the substance abuse makes it possible for the patient to more effectively deal with other problems that may exist. For these and other reasons, often the most crucial decision that the clinician will make is to address the substance abuse first, directly, and firmly (Khantzian, 1985; Levin, 1987; Steinglass et al.; Vannicelli, 1982; Vannicelli, Dillavou, & Caplan, 1988; Zimberg, 1982).

Treatment options today are extensive and include a wide array of inpatient and outpatient programs of varying lengths and intensity. Although clinical research has not documented the superiority of the more costly and restrictive inpatient option over the less costly and more flexible alternative of outpatient treatment (Miller & Hester, 1986; Saxe et al., 1983), clinical judgment often points to inpatient treatment when withdrawal becomes complicated or when outpatient treatment has not proven effective. In our experience we have found that outpatient group psychotherapy is often extremely effective in supporting and facilitating the long-term work of recovery (Vannicelli, 1982, 1987), and that group psychotherapy offers the alcoholic patient many of the same kinds of advantages (Griefen, Vannicelli, & Canning, 1985; Vannicelli, 1982; Vannicelli, Canning, & Griefen, 1984; Vannicelli et al. 1988) that we have discussed for the ACOA. We also believe that AA and NA are highly synergistic with good professional treatment, and that patients should be encouraged to use these self-help programs. Patients' initial resistance can often be addressed by examining obstacles to participation. Individual, family, and couples therapy are also often extremely helpful. Finally, disulfiram (antabuse) treatment can also be a very useful adjunct to assist in impulse control during the early stages of recovery. (See Annotated Bibliography at the end of this chapter for a guide to reading about alcoholism and substance abuse.)

Information about the Alcoholic Family

Understanding what it means to grow up in an "alcoholic family" is obviously at the heart of our work with ACOAs. But it is important to be familiar with the tremendous diversity that exists among alcoholic families. Until recently the accepted view of alcoholism and the alcoholic family had been based largely on the relatively few alcoholics who found their way into treatment. By broadening our knowledge base and by understanding the ways in which alcohol may be used in the family systems of those who never reach treatment for their alcoholism, we broaden our sense of what our ACOA patients may have experienced.

The work of Steinglass and his colleagues (Steinglass et al., 1987; Wolin, Bennett, & Noonan, 1979) documents the ways in which alcohol is used by the entire family system and the ways in which it may (or may not) be entwined in the life and rituals of the family. This work also helps us to understand intergenerational transmission and identity issues around alcoholism, as well as the centrality (or lack thereof) of the "ACOA" identity.

ACOA Education

The reader who wishes to supplement his reading on psychotherapy with ACOAs will find three papers particularly helpful (Brown & Beletsis, 1986; Cermak & Brown, 1982; Hibbard, 1987). The first two articles are useful in highlighting some of the themes and issues that may be particularly salient with this population, the third in pointing out important areas of overlap between ACOAs and other clinical populations. Three recent clinical texts on the treatment of ACOAs are also available (Brown, 1988; Lewis & Williams, 1986; Wood, 1987). Finally, Robin Norwood's book, *Women Who Love Too Much,* presents a clinician's sensitive understanding of women from dysfunctional families, many of whom are the adult children of alcoholics.

In addition, since many patients who present for treatment as ACOAs have sampled from the vast self-help literature available, the therapist may want to be familiar with some of these as well (Ackerman, 1986, 1987; Black, 1981, 1985; Cermak, 1985; Friel & Friel, 1988; Gravitz & Bowden, 1985; Greenleaf, 1981; Kritsberg, 1985; McConnell, 1980, 1986; McDonnell & Callahan, 1987; Middelton-Moz & Dwinell, 1986; Miller & Ripper, 1988; Seixas & Youcha, 1985; Smith, 1988; Wegscheider-Cruse, 1984,

1985; Whitfield, 1987; Woititz, 1983, 1985). In our experience, ACOAs often find these books extremely helpful. They feel personally connected to and identify with the ideas, and in many instances these readings have also been instrumental in getting them into treatment. That the ideas expressed in these lay books are broad enough that many non-ACOA patients (and probably most of their therapists as well) will also identify with them, in no way lessens the impact on a particular ACOA client who finds these readings useful. These books are intended for the lay public and for that audience have considerable appeal. However, they should be read with a grain of salt by the therapist looking for "factual information" about ACOAs, since overgeneralizations and somewhat stereotyped characterizations are pervasive in this literature. Since the content of these books overlap considerably, it probably makes most sense to choose whichever books are most available or those which your clients seem to be talking about the most.

Group Psychotherapy Preparation

The group therapist undertaking this enterprise, ideally, will have prior training and experience in group therapy with more generic populations, before taking on his first ACOA group. Because ACOA therapy groups tend, as we have indicated, to get off to a faster and more intense start, and to create more complicated transference (and countertransference) experiences, we do not recommend initiating one's group therapy career in this way. Formal training in group psychotherapy may be accomplished via a number of routes. Clinical graduate programs in psychology, social work, and many allied disciplines often offer course work in group psychotherapy. In addition, the local divisions of the American Group Psychotherapy Association (both state and regional), offer one-, two-, and three-year training programs in group psychotherapy. Excellent textbooks on outpatient group psychotherapy include those authored by Yalom (1975), Bion (1961), and Rutan and Stone (1984).

Finally, hands-on *supervised* experience is essential. We do not recommend that even an experienced therapist begin his first

ACOA group totally on his own. The level of supervision or supervisory consultation will depend on the general level of clinical expertise of the therapist and, in particular, amount of prior experience doing group psychotherapy. Experienced therapists who are knowledgeable about group psychotherapy with other populations may wish to simply begin this enterprise with peer supervision (i.e., collaborating with a colleague who is also doing ACOA psychotherapy group). Collaboration with an experienced co-therapist may be sufficient if a provision is made for backup consultation for the occasional impasses that may develop. Therapists embarking on this venture with less group psychotherapy experience are advised to have regular supervision (weekly or biweekly), either individually or in a supervision group. While individual supervision provides greater opportunity for regular and continuous monitoring of the therapist's own particular group, the supervision group provides an opportunity to learn by listening to the snafus and glitches encountered in other groups (as well as their resolution). The former format may be less anxiety provoking initially, particularly when the therapist feels somewhat pressed about staying on top of the process in her own group (and anxious about the prospect of many observers witnessing the rough spots encountered along the way.) As competence grows, however, the group supervision format has much to recommend it, since "parallel process" often develops in the supervision group, paralleling the issues and conflicts in members' own individual groups, and providing a particularly rich arena for exploring countertransference phenomena.

Annotated Bibliography of Substance-Abuse Readings

American Psychiatric Association. *Diagnostic and statistical manual of mental disorders (3rd ed., Rev.).* Washington, DC: American Psychiatric Association, 1987. (pp. 116–185)

> These sections of DSM-III-R contain very useful descriptive information. Intoxication and withdrawal are detailed for alcohol, cocaine, marijuana, barbiturates, PCP, and other drugs. Other drug-related states such as alcohol hallucinocis, cocaine delirium, and cannabis delusional disorder, are defined. The sections providing

diagnostic criteria for the various psychoactive substance-use disorders reflect an increased recognition of the importance of psychosocial factors in determining dependence. A very useful reference.

Bader, M.J. Looking for addictions in all the wrong places. *Tikkun,* 1988, *3*(6), 13–16

A thoughtful article that examines important conceptual weaknesses and clinical pitfalls embedded in the ACOA self-help literature.

Blane, H.T., and **Leonard, K.E.** (Eds). *Psychological theories of drinking and alcoholism.* New York: Guilford, 1987.

An authoritative account of current theory and programmatic research regarding alcoholism. This book provides a stimulating array of points of view. Each chapter presents a theoretical conceptualization, research findings which bear upon it, and an assessment of its strengths and weaknesses. This is an important book for a field which is too often stifled by adherence to unchallenged beliefs.

Brown, S., and **Yalom, I.** Interactional group psychotherapy with alcoholics. *Journal of Studies on Alcohol,* 1977, *38*(3), 426-456.

The authors explain their use of interactional group psychotherapy with alcoholics. Some important issues and themes that arise in treatment are discussed. Empirical findings from their study indicate that alcoholic patients stand to gain as much as neurotic patients from this mode of therapy.

Brownell, K.D., Marlatt, G.A, Lichtenstein, E., and **Wilson, G.T.** Understanding and preventing relapse. *American Psychologist,* 1986, *41*, 765-782.

Written by cognitive behaviorists, this article looks at relapse from a psychological rather than biomedical point of view. Knowledge gained from the study of several kinds of addictive disorders (alcoholism, smoking, and obesity) is examined for commonalities.

Cook, D.R. Craftsman versus professional: Analysis of the controlled drinking controversy. *Journal of Studies on Alcohol,* 1985, *46,* 433-442.

An attempt to understand and depolarize the controversy centered on the Sobells' controlled drinking study and criticism of their conclusions by Pendry et al. (*Science,* 1985, *217,* 169-175).

Donovan, D.M., and **Marlatt, G.A.** Assessment of expectancies and behaviors associated with alcohol consumption. *Journal of Studies on Alcohol,* 1980, *41,* 1153-1185.

The authors take a systematic look at the research data bearing on many of the old saws and myths in the field of alcoholism — in particular regarding tension reduction theories of alcoholism, loss of control, craving, and mood changes and other psychological conditions during the course of alcoholism.

Donovan, J.M. An etiologic model of alcoholism. *American Journal of Psychiatry*, 1986, *143*, 1-11.

The author argues that failure to fully consider the multidimensional nature of the etiology of alcoholism has prevented research efforts from adequately integrating the contributions of heredity, environment, and psychopathology in a unified etiological model. He presents an outline of a multidimensional etiological model based on existing research findings.

Goodwin, D.W. Alcoholism and genetics: The sins of the fathers. *Archives of General Psychiatry*, 1985, *42*, 171-174.

This brief article is a good overview of what we can and cannot conclude about genetic influences in the etiology of alcoholism.

Johnson Institute. *How to use intervention in your professional practice.* Minneapolis: Johnson Institute Books, 1987.

An excellent small book. It offers the best practical guidance for facilitating an intervention by family and friends designed to make a substance-abusing loved one aware of the gravity of the problem and to motivate him or her to obtain treatment.

Khantzian, E.J. Psychotherapeutic interventions with substance abusers — The clinical context. *Journal of Substance Abuse Treatment*, 1985, *2*, 83-88.

Takes the position that ego deficits in the ability to tolerate painful affect and self-care capacities characterize many substance abusers. Suggests implications for treatment.

Kissin, B. Theory and practice in the treatment of alcoholism. In B. Kissin and H. Begleiter (Eds.), *The biology of alcoholism: (Vol. 5) Treatment and rehabilitation of the chronic alcoholic.* New York: Plenum, 1977, 1-48.

A classic, if somewhat overwhelming, overview of the biopsychosocial model of alcoholism.

Marlatt, G.A. Relapse prevention: Theoretical rationale and overview of the model In G. Marlatt and J. Gordon (Eds.), *Relapse prevention:*

maintenance strategies in addictive behavior change. New York: Guilford, 1985.

> The first chapter in an impressive book presenting a cognitive-behavioral understanding of addiction and its treatment. The best single source on the relapse-prevention model.

Mendelson, J.H., and Mello, N.K. *The diagnosis and treatment of alcoholism.* New York: McGraw-Hill, 1986. (pp. 7, 10, 197-205, 221-231)

> The indicated sections address the physiological and clinical features of alcohol dependence; and the variability of the syndrome, of the population, and of existing treatment methods.

Miller, W.R. Motivational interviewing with problem drinkers. *Behavioral Psychotherapy*, 1983, *11*, 147-172.

> An entertaining and provocative paper that defines "denial" as an interactional phenomenon and describes an approach to interviewing aimed at enhancing motivation for change.

Miller, W.R., and Hester, R.K. Inpatient alcoholism treatment: Who benefits? *American Psychologist*, 1986, *41*, 794-805.

> Treatment outcome research is reviewed in order to compare the relative effectiveness of inpatient versus outpatient treatment.

Polich, J.M., Armor, D.J., and Braiker, H.B. Patterns of alcoholism over four years. *Journal of Studies on Alcohol*, 1980, *41*, 397-416.

> This paper is based on the famous Rand Corporation follow-up study of alcoholics after treatment, which found the course of alcoholism to be variable across patients and suggested that more than one kind of remission might be possible. As such, it sparked controversy about whether controlled drinking might be a viable treatment goal.

Sobell, L.C., Sobell, M.B., and Nirenberg, T.D. Behavioral assessment and treatment planning with alcohol and drug abusers: A review with an emphasis on clinical application. *Clinical Psychology Review*, 1988, *8*, 19-54.

> Lists the types of information useful in a functional analysis of alcohol and drug use. Reviews a wide variety of assessment tools. Emphasizes a close relationship between assessment and treatment planning.

Vannicelli, M. Group therapy with alcoholics: Special techniques. *Journal of Studies on Alcohol,* 1982, *43,* 17-37.

Identifies key issues and technical problems that arise in the interactional group treatment of substance abusers. Practical interventions are suggested which enable the clinician to respond effectively.

Vannicelli, M., Canning, D., and **Griefen, M.** Group therapy with alcoholics: A group case study. *International Journal of Group Psychotherapy,* 1984, *34,* 127-147.

Companion paper to the Vannicelli 1982 article, it presents detailed clinical examples of the techniques described, by examining their use in a long-term group over the course of two years.

Weiss, R.D., and **Mirin, S.M.** Substance abuse as an attempt at self-medication. *Psychiatric Medicine,* 1987, *3,* 357-367.

Stresses the heterogeneity of the substance-abusing population and advises that several weeks of observation after the patient is drug free may be needed to assess possible premorbid psychopathology.

Zucker, R.A. The four alcoholisms: A Developmental account of the etiologic process. In C. Rivers (Ed.), *Alcohol and addictive behavior: Nebraska symposium on motivation,* 1986. Lincoln: University of Nebraska Press, 1987.

Offers a model for construing the influences on etiology of alcoholism as these influences vary over the course of individuals' development. Posits a set of types of alcoholism which differ in etiology.

Zucker, R.A., and **Gomberg, E.S.L.** Etiology of alcoholism reconsidered: The case for a biopsychosocial process. *American Psychologist,* 1986, *41,* 783-793.

Reviews longitudinal research on the etiology of alcoholism. Contrary to the increasingly prevalent view that alcoholism is predominantly a biological and genetic phenomenon, it concludes that childhood, personality, and cultural influences are important factors in the etiology of alcoholism.

10
Research Perspectives and Future Directions

Although group psychotherapy is currently being widely used with ACOA populations, there is very little solid data documenting its effectiveness. In an extensive review of ACOA literature through 1987 (abstract searches from the National Clearing House for Alcohol information, Journal of Studies on Alcohol, and the National Library of Medicine's MEDLINE Data Base), only two studies were found that examined the effectiveness of group psychotherapy with this population (Peitler, 1980; Barnard & Spoentgen, 1986a — also described in less detail in Barnard and Spoentgen 1986b.)

Peitler compared the effectiveness of group psychotherapy and Alateen* with respect to their impact on feelings of self-worth, withdrawal tendencies, and antisocial tendencies. He randomly assigned two groups of male adolescents — those who were age seven or younger when father's alcoholism became apparent and those who were older than seven — to one of three treatment groups: group counseling, Alateen, and a control group which received no treatment. He found that the group counseling was more effective, in general, than Alateen for both age groups. Moreover, he found that Alateen's effectiveness in improving the adjustment of this population along the dimensions considered was no better than no treatment (the control group), with the exception of the younger onset group which showed significant increases in feelings of self-worth following participation in Alateen.

---

*Al-Anon Meeting for teenagers.

The Barnard and Spoentgen 1986a study examined (1) adult children of nonalcoholic parents, (2) ACOAs who were not currently seeking treatment, and (3) ACOAs who were currently requesting to participate in an ACOA "educational/supportive" treatment group. The experimental group (ACOAs receiving the group therapy intervention) showed significantly more improvement in psychological functioning between the pretest (prior to the group intervention) and the posttest (following the eighth session of the group) than did the nontreatment-seeking ACOAs during the same time period. The areas of improvement following the group psychotherapy intervention included: greater tendency toward inner-directedness, higher self-regard, greater capacity for intimate contact with others, and reduction in other-directedness. Thus, this study provides suggestive data regarding the effectiveness of at least short-term group interventions with ACOAs.

This study is also important in documenting that ACOAs cannot be uniformly assumed to be impaired people in need of treatment. Barnard and Spoentgen found, in fact, that the treatment-seeking ACOAs were significantly different from both the non-ACOA college students and the ACOA college students who were not seeking treatment. The two latter groups, nontreatment-seeking ACOAs and "normal" controls, in fact, differed on only one dimension, "capacity for intimate contact with others," with the nontreatment-seeking ACOAs having a *greater* capacity for intimate contact than the non-ACOAs. (The treatment-seeking ACOAs, as might be expected, showed a significantly poorer capacity for developing intimate contact with others than either of the other two groups; and on several other dimensions also scored more poorly.)

Several other recent studies (Barnes, Benson, & Wilsnack, 1979; Beardslee, Son, & Vaillant, 1986; Benson & Heller, 1987; Jacob & Leonard, 1986; Wolin et al., 1979) suggest that caution is indicated regarding generalizations about the negative impact of having grown up in an alcoholic family. These studies are supported by thoughtful commentary by Brown (1988), Burk and Sher (1988), Russell et al. (1985), Wilson and Orford (1978), and Wood (1987), suggesting that ACOAs may be more resilient than might be suggested by much of the popular ACOA press.

Jacob and Leonard (1986) carefully compared children of

alcoholic, depressed, and control (social drinking, nondepressed) fathers, on both teacher and parent ratings. Although the children of alcoholics and of depressives were rated higher on behavior problems than the children of controls, only a minority of children in either group received scores indicative of severe impairment. In addition, contrary to expectation, the most severe problems were found in daughters of depressed (rather than alcoholic) fathers.

Barnes et al. (1979), in a college sample, compared daughters of alcoholic fathers with daughters of nonalcoholic fathers. As expected, they found that the young women who had alcoholic fathers drank more than did those whose fathers were not alcoholic and, also, experienced more drinking-related problems. However, their data did not support the hypothesis that the two groups would differ on depression, sex-role characteristics or sexual behavior. Preliminary analyses suggested that severity of father's alcoholism, daughter's age when father's drinking problems began, daughter's age when first aware of her father's alcoholism, and daughter's own drinking problem were important factors in the eventual adjustment of these female ACOAs.

Beardslee et al. (1986), in a study comparing males who had grown up with an alcoholic parent to males growing up without exposure to parental alcoholism, supported the findings of Barnes and his associates with female subjects. Again, they found that degree of exposure to parental alcoholism related significantly to alcoholism and alcohol-related problems in later life (more specifically, to alcohol use, alcoholism, time in jail, sociopathy, and death). However, in contrast to what might be expected from much of the clinical literature, degree of exposure to parental alcoholism was not significantly related to measures of adult ego-functioning or to physical health or rates of unemployment. Moreover, most of the impairment observed in ACOAs occurred in those subjects who actually developed alcoholism. The authors conclude about the ACOAs in this study, "The majority of youngsters in this sample function similarly to those in the non-exposed group during adulthood, in spite of the severe alcoholism and discord in the families in which they grew up" (p. 590).

Benson and Heller (1987), in their study of the adjustment status of women whose fathers were alcoholic compared to those whose fathers were psychiatrically disturbed or normal, also found results consistent with those of Barnes et al. (1979). While daughters of both alcoholic (or problem-drinking) fathers and psychiatrically disturbed fathers reported more neurotic and acting-out symptomotology than did daughters of normal fathers, daughters of psychiatrically disturbed and alcoholic fathers did not differ from each other. Moreover, daughters of the psychiatrically disturbed fathers actually fared worse than those of alcoholic fathers in terms of higher scores on depression. Rates of alcohol use among the three groups of daughters in this study did not differ.

While this study points to increased disturbance among daughters of drinking fathers, it also points out that level of disturbance was not unique to this group, but rather, was similar to that found among daughters of emotionally disturbed fathers. The investigators conclude, "daughters generally were more likely to report symptomatology if their fathers were described as psychologically disturbed, regardless of the type of disturbance" (p. 309). In attempting to reconcile their findings with clinical reports of unique psychological damage to children growing up in an alcoholic home, Benson and Heller point to the fact that the clinical literature consists primarily of anecdotal case studies, with comparison groups, if used at all, limited to normal controls. With this kind of limited data, faulty conclusions may be drawn about the unique effects of growing up in an alcoholic family. The picture that emerges more and more is that family dysfunction is one important factor in the development of a healthy (or unhealthy) adult, but that even when family dysfunction exists, there may be remediating factors that may lead to the development of relatively well-adjusted adults.

Wolin and Steinglass, and their associates (Steinglass et al., 1987; Wolin et al., 1979) have systematically investigated one such "remitting factor" that may protect the ACOA from some of the potentially negative effects of growing up in an alcoholic family. In particular, their studies look at the intergenerational transmission of alcoholism — the extent to which children raised in alcoholic families either become alcoholic themselves, or marry substance-abusing partners. More specifically, they find that when family rituals remain intact and are not altered during periods of heaviest parental drinking, that alcoholism and alcohol-related problems are less likely to be transmitted into the children's generation. (This is in contrast to families in which alcoholism becomes an important component of family rituals — where the message to growing children is, presumably, that the continuance of family identity in subsequent generations can only be insured if alcoholism, itself, is perpetuated. Differentiating between "distinctive families" in which the alcoholism remains compartmentalized and walled off and "subsumptive families" in which the alcoholism has a diffused impact, invading "virtually every nook and cranny of family life" (p. 310), they suggest that distinctive families are less "alcoholic" than subsumptive families.

These studies suggest that care must be exercised in assuming that all ACOAs are damaged or in need of treatment. It would appear that some (perhaps many) ACOAs thrive *despite* adverse familial circumstances, or perhaps manifest greater resilience precisely *because of* the experience of growing up in an alcoholic family. Studies of resilient children who appear to cope in the face of adversity (Rutter, 1979; Werner, 1986) cite a number of factors that may mediate a child's response to stress and help us to understand positive adaptations that may emerge.

Rutter, reviewing a series of studies of heterogeneous samples of children, identified four factors mediating the effects of maternal deprivation: (1) individual characteristics of the child (temperament, sex and coping skills); (2) factors within the family (alternative supportive parent figures); (3) environmental factors (characteristics of school and neighborhood); and (4) multiplicity of stresses and the effect of one stressor in potentiating the damage caused by others. Werner, studying specifically the adult children of alcoholic parents, confirmed the importance of individual characteristics of the child (temperament, intelligence, achievement orientation, positive self-esteem, and internal locus of control) in creating resilience to family dysfunction. In addition she pointed to mediating factors in the care-giving environment, such as adequate attention from the primary care-giver during infancy and absence of prolonged separation; no additional births during the first two years of childhood (potentially averting adequate attention); and the absence of conflict between the parents during the first two years of life.

In addition to research data documenting the fallacy of

assuming that all ACOAs are "disturbed people in need of treatment" and pointing to the tremendous variability in resilience among the ACOA population, there is also increasing data documenting the considerable overlap between the kinds of dysfunction seen in troubled alcoholic families and other kinds of dysfunctional families. Orford (1975) systematically reviews this body of literature, pointing to studies that show considerable similarity between alcoholic families and other dysfunctional or stressed families in terms of: anxiety and insecurity, social isolation, absence of clear guidelines for reactions, and role transfer from one family member to another — leading him to conclude,

> Marriages complicated by alcoholism are exposed to a potentially crisis-producing series of events. But many of the reactions which then take place are shared by members of families exposed to other, seemingly quite different, sets of stressful events. (p. 1541)

The overlap that Orford so clearly documents is supported by a number of research studies. Billings, Kessler, Gomberg, and Weiner (1979), comparing the marital interactions of alcoholic couples and nonalcoholic maritally distressed couples, found them to be similarly impaired. As expected, the interactions of both the alcoholic couples and the distressed couples were more problematic than were the interactions of the control (nonalcoholic and nondistressed) couples. Similarly, Moos, and Moos (1984) found that the family environments of recovering alcoholics resembled those of community controls along a number of dimensions. These data, taken as a whole, support the premise that, while many alcoholic families are dysfunctional in significant ways, the dysfunction is not unique to them.

In terms of future directions for research, the studies above point to the need for greater precision in defining ACOAs in the research that remains to be carried out. Certainly a distinction needs to be made between ACOAs who seek treatment and ACOAs who are not seeking treatment. Along with this, a number of variables need to be explored to help us better understand why some ACOAs may suffer greater impairment while others (presumably more resilient to the influences of an alcoholic parent) may suffer less. Such factors would include the following: (1) subtype, duration, and severity of alcoholism; (2) whether one or both parents were alcoholic; (3) the effect of recovery of parent(s) from alcoholism, as opposed to temporary abstinence; (4) extent of alcoholism in the extended family network; (5) whether the alcoholic parent was the same sex or opposite sex of the child; (6) how old the child was during the period of severe drinking problems; (7) whether other drug problems were present in the family; (8) whether there was other serious psychiatric psychopathology in the family; (9) whether there was physical or sexual abuse in the family; (10) whether there was serious neglect of the children; (11) whether there was serious shortage in the family resources for basic survival (adequate finances, shelter, food); (12) the extent to which family alcoholism was subsumptive versus distinctive. In addition, strengths inherent in the family network would need to be considered including availability of other resources during the stressful drinking periods (supportive grandparents, a healthy nondrinking parent, presence of other parent surrogates) and the extent to which family life was organized and predictable, despite the presence of alcohol.

Thus, research attempts to learn more about the effectiveness of group psychotherapy with adult children of alcoholics will involve, initially, a more careful definition of the ACOA population and subgroups. Once this is done, we will be in a better position to ask how effective group psychotherapy is (as opposed to other treatment modalities) for various subgroups of ACOAs. We will need to know more about the outcome of therapy groups compared to: (1) no treatment, (2) individual treatment, (3) self-help groups, or (4) therapy groups in combination with either individual treatment or self-help groups.

We will also need to know more about the parameters of group treatment itself that influence its effectiveness, including: (1) duration of the group (short-term versus long-term), (2) orientation of the group (psychodynamic versus psychoeducational versus supportive); (3) open group (in which new members join as older members graduate) versus closed group (in which membership is fixed and all members join and terminate together) (4) same versus mixed sex group; and (5) homogeneous versus heterogeneous membership (i.e., demographic match of members with regard to sex, age, marital status, education, etc.). Another important group parameter that needs greater attention is the group culture itself — its stability, ability to accept new members, group openness and trust — and the way in which the group culture influences the clinical outcomes of particular subgroups of ACOAs. Finally, it would be instructive to know more about the impact of various leader characteristics on the group culture (and, ultimately, on outcome) for specific subgroups of ACOAs. Thus, studies are needed of the impact of leader style, training, discipline, and level of skill on the group culture that develops. Also useful would be studies that compare the impact of a single leader versus a co-leader team, and the effect of having an ACOA leader versus a non-ACOA leader (as well as a combination of the two).

Because some patients are better able to "connect" to a group than are others, it would also be instructive to know more about the particular characteristics that make this connection possible — that is, those personal characteristics that differentiate patients who agree to join from those who refuse. Similarly, it would help to know why, once in a group, some patients are more likely than others to continue membership and to come regularly. More information is also needed about the characteristics that differentiate subgroups of ACOAs in terms of their ability to tolerate adverse conditions in the group (such as leader turnover, member turnover, less skilled group leaders). And most important, of those who remain in group, patients vary in their ability to productively use it. Thus, studies are needed that focus on those particular personal attributes and strengths that enable a patient to use group therapy most effectively and those areas of change (outcome dimensions) that are linked to specific patient characteristics.

Finally, systematic study is needed of countertransference phenomena as they manifest themselves in the group leader's behavior. More specifically, this might include studies of frequency, intensity, and/or quality of countertransference slippage that may differentiate ACOA from non-ACOA therapy groups — and, in particular, differentiating ACOA groups where the group leaders are themselves ACOAs. Having adequately investigated and more systematically catalogued countertransference phenomena when working with the ACOA population, we would then be in a position to explore the impact of countertransference training on leader skill and clinical outcome with ACOAs.

In closing, it is hoped that the reader will carry away a sense of direction and purpose in conducting group psychotherapy with adult children of alcoholics. To expedite an effective journey in this direction, I have pointed out trends, themes, and commonalities that may serve as guides along the way. It is equally important to remember, however, that there are many differences among ACOAs and that the effectiveness of group treatment generally, as well as the specific clinical strategies and interventions proposed, is bound to vary considerably from one ACOA member to the next. Although it may be useful to consider similarities and trends it is essential not to lose sight of the tremendous diversity among the people that we label ACOAs.

Conclusion

We began this journey with a series of questions. These questions have influenced the course that we have taken and the points of interest that I have called attention to along the way. Although frequently the answers were more complex than the questions themselves, and punctuated by qualifiers and modifiers, as we near the end it may be helpful to recapitulate these initial issues and summarize briefly the territory that we have covered.

We began by inquiring about the "core constellation" of the ACOA "syndrome" — asking what "the typical ACOA" might look like. We reviewed the many diverse constellations of characteristics, (more than 30 in all) put forth by many writers in this field, and pointed to the considerable overlap between these lists of characteristics and the kind of symptoms and problems that patients, across a variety of diagnostic groups, present with for treatment. We have pointed, throughout, to the tremendous heterogeneity within the ACOA population and to the considerable overlap between ACOAs and many other people whose current problems relate to issues in their families of origin.

We then asked whether all (or even most) ACOAs need treatment. In paying attention to the tremendous heterogeneity among this population, we have also pointed to a growing body of research documenting that children from chaotic, dysfunctional families often develop strengths and adaptations that serve them well in later life. The growing literature on resilient children gives us much to think about in this regard. Although most writers in this field — both those writing for lay audiences and those writing for more clinical audiences, acknowledge that many ACOAs "look" highly adaptive, functional, and successful, the popular (though unsubstantiated) view is that if you scratch the surface of these "so-called" adaptive, successful people, pathology and maladaptation will be apparent. This is a view that has little to support it, and, in fact, runs counter not only to good common sense, but also to solid clinical thinking. After all, among the many ways that we measure mental health are the very signifiers that we notice in some ACOAs — ability to work hard and to achieve professional and career goals, ability to assume responsibility and to carry a job to completion, and capacity for intimacy. To argue that all of these strengths are merely "defensive adaptations" is hardly in keeping with good clinical thinking. Moreover, as Burk and Sher (1988) point out, the very notion that all ACOAs are basically impaired people in need of treatment, and an over-emphasis on labeling, may actually serve a dysfunctional purpose for those ACOAs who are functioning quite well. The ACOA who is happy and satisfied with his life is in no greater need of self-scrutiny (or scrutiny by others) than any of the rest of us. As these authors point out, such scrutiny may, in the long run even be potentially detrimental.

The question about the relative health of ACOAs compared to other populations entering outpatient clinics was addressed by considering, again, the tremendous heterogeneity of this population. After all, it is possible to be an adult child of an alcoholic and simultaneously be classified as belonging to virtually any diagnostic category — ranging from the most disturbed forms of psychopathology to the healthier adaptations of the "normal" person.

With regard to the kind of psychotherapy that might be indicated for this population, I indicated a strong personal bias towards group psychotherapy and listed many of the possible advantages to the ACOA of being in a group with other adult children of alcoholics. However, as I also pointed out, neither the group therapy nor any other kind of therapy that might be used with ACOAs, needs to — or even should — vary significantly from the kind of work that we do with other patients. We can assume that most of our patients (non-ACOAs as well as ACOAs) come from families that were in some way or another "dysfunctional," and, thinking from a psychodynamic perspective, we also assume that for most of our patients the problems in living that they now deal with relate in some substantial way to issues in their families of origin.

As to whether ACOAs can be treated in generic psychotherapy groups or are more appropriately handled in specialty groups with other ACOAs, again, I indicated my own preferences in this regard — pointing to some of the advantages of putting people together who have identified around this common issue. However, as I also indicated, the kinds of issues that emerge are not unique to this population and would be addressed by a sensitive therapist in any psychodynamically oriented group — even if other members were not ACOAs.

With regard to the concept of "recovery," we are addressing a more complicated question. Clearly the term "recovery" has a special meaning when we are talking about substance abuse. In common parlance, the term "recovery" refers to abstinence from alcohol and drugs, and the changes or improvements in one's life that go along with this. When we speak of ACOAs, the concept of "recovery" is considerably more complicated. After all, how does one "recover" from the illness of one's parent? How does one recover from having had an alcoholic or a manic-depressive or a schizophrenic parent, or obsessive-compulsive parent? Clearly, from a clinical standpoint, our notion of therapeutic growth with ACOAs will not differ substantially from our notion of growth with any other clinical population. Growth is marked by feeling better about oneself, and by functioning in the world in a way that is more consistent with one's goals, values, and resources. The same is true for the ACOA.

With regard to the particular stance appropriate for the ACOA therapist, again, I have tried to make the point that good psychotherapy is also good ACOA psychotherapy. A sensitive clinician listens to the issues that his patients bring and addresses them on a case by case basis, responding to the specific needs of each particular patient. However, I also highlighted the importance of being tuned into issues connected with drinking (the patient's, as well as current significant others that he is living with), and the importance of being able to respond knowledgeably and sensitively to the patient's concerns about this.

With regard to the situation in which alcohol and drugs are currently causing problems for the patient or for those that he is living with, I have pointed to the need for the therapist to have sufficient training to be able to take an adequate alcohol and drug history and to be able to assess the need for substance-abuse treatment when this is indicated. (Although this is particularly important with regard to ACOAs, I might add that I believe it is a sine qua non of good treatment for all clinical populations.) Along with this, the ACOA therapist should be aware of resources in his area that provide treatment for substance abuse.

Special issues for the ACOA therapist who is herself an ACOA received considerable attention in this volume as we discussed some of the more important aspects of the countertransference dilemmas that might emerge. With regard to the therapist's self-disclosure about her own ACOA history (or lack thereof), we considered some of the advantages and disadvantages of self-disclosure, and the importance of understanding the meaning of the patient's request for personal information about the therapist. We also emphasized that a "simple straightforward answer" may not in fact be particularly useful, and often fails to address the patient's underlying concerns.

Finally, we addressed the special training needs of the ACOA therapist — particularly for the therapist beginning to work with ACOAs in groups. We pointed to the need for expertise not only in group psychotherapy, but also the need for knowledge and sensitivity about substance-abuse problems in general, and an understanding of the popular ACOA "beliefs" that many of our patients will enter treatment with.

In conclusion, I hope that the reader who has journeyed with me will feel, as a result, a little more familiar with the territory of group psychotherapy with ACOAs and will carry away some tools, as well as a sense of enthusiasm, for his own future journeys along this road.

APPENDIX A
ACOA Alcohol and Drug History Questionnaire

APPLETON ACOA
Alcohol and Drug History

NAME_____ INTERVIEWER: _____
   (Last)   (First)   (Middle)

Date: _____

RELATIVES' ALCOHOL/DRUG HISTORIES
Father
Has or has had alcohol/drug abuse problem: yes____ no____
If yes: abuse ongoing____ died from it____ don't know____
   recovering: number of months of total abstinence_____
   How? (AA/NA, therapy, antabuse, etc.)_____
Drug(s) of choice: alcohol____ cocaine____ cannabis____ opiate____
           minor tranquilizer____ other_____
Drinking: alcoholic____ heavy____ moderate____ little____ none____

Mother
Has or has had alcohol/drug abuse problem: yes____ no____
If yes: abuse ongoing____ died from it____ don't know____
   recovering: number of months of total abstinence_____
   How? (AA/NA, therapy, antabuse, etc.)_____
Drug(s) of choice: alcohol____ cocaine____ cannabis____ opiate____
           minor tranquilizer____ other_____
Drinking: alcoholic____ heavy____ moderate____ little____ none____

Spouse
Has or has had alcohol/drug abuse problem: yes____ no____
If yes: abuse ongoing____ died from it____ don't know____
   recovering: number of months of total abstinence_____
   How? (AA/NA, therapy, antabuse, etc.)_____
Drug(s) of choice: alcohol____ cocaine____ cannabis____ opiate____
           minor tranquilizer____ other_____
Drinking: alcoholic____ heavy____ moderate____ little____ none____

Other relatives with substance-abuse problems
(sibling, step-parent, aunt/uncle, grandparent, fiance, former spouse)

Nature of relationship_____
Recovering____ abuse ongoing____ died from it____ don't know____
Drug(s) of choice: alcohol____ cocaine____ cannabis____ opiate____
           minor tranquilizer____ other_____

Nature of relationship_____
Recovering____ abuse ongoing____ died from it____ don't know____
Drug(s) of choice: alcohol____ cocaine____ cannabis____ opiate____
      minor tranquilizer____ other_____

Nature of relationship_____
Recovering____ abuse ongoing____ died from it____ don't know____
Drug(s) of choice: alcohol____ cocaine____ cannabis____ opiate____
      minor tranquilizer____ other_____

Nature of relationship_____
Recovering____ abuse ongoing____ died from it____ don't know____
Drug(s) of choice: alcohol____ cocaine____ cannabis____ opiate____
      minor tranquilizer____ other_____

Nature of relationship_____
Recovering____ abuse ongoing____ died from it____ don't know____
Drug(s) of choice: alcohol____ cocaine____ cannabis____ opiate____
      minor tranquilizer____ other_____

RECENT ALCOHOL/DRUG HISTORY

When was last drink/drug use? _____
If no longer using, why stopped alcohol/drug use? _____
_____

If recent increase in use, was there an identifiable precipitant? yes____ no____
    no sudden increase____ If yes, describe:_____
_____

Alcohol/drug use during past year:

	Average days/week	Quantity/day
Alcohol..................		
Cocaine		
Cannabis................		
Other:____		
Other:____		
Other:____		

Predominant pattern of drinking/drug use during past year: light social____ heavy
    social____ binge____ maintenance____
Social context of drinking/drug use (past year):
    alone____ with others____ home____ work____ social settings____
Used alcohol with other CNS depressants (e.g., Valium, opiates): yes____ no____
    If presently employed or a student:
        # days missed due to substance use in month prior to treatment_____
        # days left early or arrived late due to substance use in month prior to
        treatment_____
        # days in past 3 years missed work or school because of substance
        use_____

PAST SUBSTANCE USE HISTORY

Age of first drink_____   Age of onset of heaviest drinking_____
Age of first drug use_____   Age of onset of heaviest drug use_____

Identifiable precipitant of changes in pattern (or onset of alcohol/drug use?
   yes____ no____ If yes, describe:_____
Longest alcohol-and-drug-free period in heaviest drinking/drug use years____
Longest drug-of-choice-free period in heaviest drinking/drug use years _____
Alcohol/drug use during heaviest one month period (age=_____):

	Average days/week	Quantity/day
Alcohol................		
Cocaine................		
Cannabis...............		
Other:_____		
Other:_____		
Other:_____		

Include minor tranquilizers, opiates, etc. (even if prescribed).
Use specific names of "other" drugs.
For *Quantity*: give representative range, specify IV use, freebase.

SYMPTOMS

Alcohol-related symptoms:

	Age first noticed	Number of occurrences in past year
Blackouts		
Memory deficit...............		
Tremors (shakes).............		
Hallucinations.................		
Numbness		
Uncoordination		
Blurred vision		
Other:_____		
Other:_____		

Check if no alcohol-related symptoms__

Drug-related symptoms:

	Age first noticed	Number of occurrences in past year
Tremors (shakes).............		
Profuse sweating.............		
Nausea		
Vomiting......................		

	Age first noticed	Number of occurrences in past year
Dry heaves......................		
Poor appetite		
Weight loss		
Diarrhea		
Seeing things not there		
Hearing voices		
Feeling things under skin ..		
Seizures; convulsions		
Insomnia......................		
Other:_____		
Other:_____		

Check if no drug-related symptoms___

LEGAL PROBLEMS

Number of arrests *directly related to drinking or drug use* (e.g., DWI, drunk and disorderly, possession, dealing): past year_____ total_____
Specific types of charges:_____
Number of *other* arrests: past year_____ total_____
Specific types of charges:_____

Illicit methods used to obtain or pay for drugs: dealing____ theft____
prostitution____ other:_____ none____

PREVIOUS TREATMENT

Substance Abuse Treatment

Outpatient treatment

	Number of times used				Age ranges when treatment occurred
	None	1-5	6-20	21+	
Substance-abuse counseling					
Group therapy					
Antabuse......................					
Naltraxone					
AA/NA_____					
Other:_____					
Other:					

Inpatient treatment
Total number of hospitalizations_____ Duration of longest_____
Age ranges when treatment occurred_____

Other Psychiatric Treatment:

Outpatient Treatment

	Number of times used				Age ranges when treatment occurred
	None	1-5	6-20	21+	
Individual therapy............					
Group therapy					
Couple/family therapy					
Behavioral therapy...........					
Other:_____					
Other:_____					

Major tranquilizers ever? yes____ no____   Treatment for (circle): depression; panic/anxiety; sexual abuse; eating disorder

Anti-depressants ever? yes____ no____

Inpatient treatment
Total number of hospitalizations_____ Duration of longest_____
Age ranges when treatment occurred_____

APPENDIX B
Michigan Alcoholism Screening Test and Scoring Key

QUESTIONNAIRE ABOUT DRINKING PROBLEMS

Directions: If a statement says something true about you, put a check ( ) in the nearby space under YES. If a statement says something not true about you, put a check in the nearby space under NO. Please answer all the questions.

		YES	NO
1.	Do you feel you are a normal drinker?	____	____
2.	Have you ever awakened the morning after some drinking the night before and found that you could not remember a part of that evening?	____	____
3.	Does your spouse (or parents) ever worry or complain about your drinking?	____	____
4.	Can you stop drinking without a struggle after one or two drinks?	____	____
5.	Do you ever feel bad about your drinking?	____	____
6.	Do friends or relatives think you are a normal drinker?	____	____
7.	Do you ever try to limit your drinking to certain times of the day or to certain places?	____	____
8.	Are you always able to stop drinking when you want to?	____	____
9.	Have you ever attended a meeting of Alcoholics Anonymous (AA)?	____	____
10.	Have you gotten into fights when drinking?	____	____
11.	Has drinking ever created problems with you and your spouse?	____	____
12.	Has your spouse (or other family member) ever gone to anyone for help about your drinking?	____	____
13.	Have you ever lost friends or girlfriends or boyfriends because of your drinking?	____	____
14.	Have you ever gotten into trouble at work because of your drinking?	____	____
15.	Have you ever lost a job because of your drinking?	____	____

	YES	NO

16. Have you ever neglected your obligations, your family or your work for two or more days in a row because you were drinking?   _____ _____

17. Do you ever drink before noon?   _____ _____

18. Have you ever been told you have liver trouble?   _____ _____

19. Have you ever had delirium tremens (DTs), severe shaking, heard voices or seen things that weren't there after heavy drinking?   _____ _____

20. Have you ever gone to anyone for help about your drinking?   _____ _____

21. Have you ever been in a hospital because of you drinking?   _____ _____

22. Have you ever been a patient in a psychiatric hospital or on a psychiatric ward of a general hospital where drinking was part of the problem?   _____ _____

23. Have you ever been seen in a psychiatric or mental health clinic, or gone to a doctor, social worker, or clergyman for help with an emotional problem in which drinking played a part?   _____ _____

24. Have you ever been arrested, even for a few hours, because of drunk behavior?   _____ _____

25. Have you ever been arrested for drunk driving or driving after drinking?   _____ _____

SCORING KEY TO MAST

Directions for scoring: Add together point values for all items on which points are earned, to classify patient as: *social drinker* (total score of 0-2 points); *borderline* (total score of 3-4 points); or *alcoholic* (total score of 5 and above).

		YES	NO
1.	Do you feel you are a normal drinker?		2
2.	Have you ever awakened the morning after some drinking the night before and found that you could not remember a part of that evening?	2	
3.	Does your spouse (or parents) ever worry or complain about your drinking?	1	
4.	Can you stop drinking without a struggle after one or two drinks?		2
5.	Do you ever feel bad about your drinking?	1	
6.	Do friends or relatives think you are a normal drinker?		2
7.	Do you ever try to limit your drinking to certain times of the day or to certain places?		
8.	Are you always able to stop drinking when you want to?		2
9.	Have you ever attended a meeting of Alcoholics Anonymous (AA)?	5*	
10.	Have you gotten into fights when drinking?	1	
11.	Has drinking ever created problems with you and your spouse?	2	
12.	Has your spouse (or other family member) ever gone to anyone for help about your drinking?	2	
13.	Have you ever lost friends or girlfriends or boyfriends because of your drinking?	2	
14.	Have you ever gotten into trouble at work because of your drinking?	2	
15.	Have you ever lost a job because of your drinking?	2	
16.	Have you ever neglected your obligations, your family or your work for two or more days in a row because you were drinking?	2	
17.	Do you ever drink before noon?	1	

---

*Discretion may be indicated in scoring this item to account for those who accompanied an alcoholic family member to a meeting.

		YES	NO
18.	Have you ever been told you have liver trouble?	2	
19.	Have you ever had delirium tremens (DTs), severe shaking, heard voices or seen things that weren't there after heavy drinking?	5	
20.	Have you ever gone to anyone for help about your drinking?	5	
21.	Have you ever been in a hospital because of your drinking?	5	
22.	Have you ever been a patient in a psychiatric hospital or on a psychiatric ward of a general hospital where drinking was part of the problem?	2	
23.	Have you ever been seen in a psychiatric or mental health clinic, or gone to a doctor, social worker, or clergyman for help with an emotional problem in which drinking played a part?	2	
24.	Have you ever been arrested, even for a few hours, because of drunk behavior?	2	
25.	Have you ever been arrested for drunk driving or driving after drinking?	2	

APPENDIX C
Group Ground Rules

APPLETON OUTPATIENT PSYCHOTHERAPY GROUP GROUND RULES

The behavior and feelings of members of the therapy group mirror in important ways behavior and feelings in other important relationships. Consequently, the group provides a setting in which to examine patterns of behavior in relationships. The group also provides a context in which members learn to identify, understand, and express their feelings. The therapist's role is to facilitate this group process.

To foster these goals, we believe that several group ground rules are important. These are as follows:

1. Members joining long-term groups remain as long as they find the group useful in working on important issues in their lives. We recommend at least a year. Members are required to make an initial three-month commitment in order to determine the usefulness of a particular group for them.

2. Regular and timely attendance at all sessions is expected. As a member, it is your responsibility to notify the group in advance when you know that you will be away or late for group. In the event of an unexpected absence, you should notify the group at least 24 hours in advance to avoid being charged for the missed session.

3. Members of Appleton substance abuse groups are committed to maintaining abstinence. If a relapse does occur, it must be discussed promptly in the group—as must thoughts or concerns about resuming drug/alcohol use. Members of ACOA and family groups are asked to be reflective about their own substance use and to bring up changes in patterns of use or concerns that may be associated with use.

4. Members will notify the group if they are considering leaving the group. Because leaving the group is a process, just as joining is, members are expected to see this process through for at least three weeks following notification of termination.

5. Members will have a commitment to talk about important issues in their lives that cause difficulty in relating to others or in living life fully.

6. Members will also have a commitment to talk about what is going on in the group itself as a way of better understanding their own interpersonal dynamics.

7. Members will treat matters that occur in the group with utmost confidentiality. To that end, members are expected not to discuss what happens in the group with people who are not members of the group.

8. Outside-of-group-contact often has considerable impact on the group's therapeutic effectiveness. Therefore, any relevant interactions between

members which occur outside the group should be brought back into the next meeting and shared with the entire group.

9. What you share in the group will be shared with other members of the treatment team when we feel that it is important to your treatment to do so.

10. Payments for group are due monthly. If for any reason timely payment becomes problematic, members are expected to discuss this in the group.

APPENDIX D
Clinical Face Sheet

CLINICAL FACE SHEET

I. PATIENT DEMOGRAPHICS

Patient Name:_____

Date of Birth:_____ Ins. Co. and #:_____

Contact Person in Case of Emergency:_____

Home Address:_____

Telephone: Home:_____ Work:_____

II. TREATMENT CONTRACT

Fee:

      Amount:_____

      Scheduling of Payments:_____

      Billing Party (Directly to Patient or to Insurance Company):_____

      Schedule for Review of Rates or Increases in Fee:_____

Length of Session:_____

Cancellation Policy:_____

_____

III. CONTACT WITH OTHER TREATERS:

      Therapist 1: Name:_____

                 Phone:_____

                 Permission to Contact: Yes/No

      Therapist 2: Name:_____

                 Phone:_____

                 Permission to Contact: Yes/No

References

Ackerman, R.J. (Ed.). (1986) *Growing in the shadow*. Pompano Beach, FL: Health Communications.

Ackerman, R.J. (1987) *Same house different homes*. Pompano Beach, FL: Health Communications.

Alpert, G. (1970). *Therapeutic effects of therapist patient matching and positive therapist expectancies*. Doctoral dissertation, Harvard University, Cambridge, MA. (University Microfilms No. 72-33398)

Alpert, G. (1988). *Rapid turnover groups: Therapist techniques for facilitating the development of productive group process*. Unpublished manuscript.

American Psychiatric Association. (1987). *Diagnostic and statistical manual of mental disorders* (3rd ed., rev.). Washington, DC: American Psychiatric Association.

Anderson, P.K. (1988). *Adult children of alcoholics: Coming home*. Seattle: Glen Abbey Books.

Bader, M.J. (1988). Looking for addictions in all the wrong places. *Tikkun 3*(6), 13–16.

Barnard, C.P., & Spoentgen, P.A. (1986a). Children of alcoholics: Characteristics and treatment. *Alcoholism Treatment Quarterly, 3*(4), 47–65.

Barnard, C.P., & Spoentgen, P.A. (1986b). Are children of alcoholics different? A research report on group process. *Focus on Family and Chemical Dependency, 9*(2), 20–22.

Barnes, J.L., Benson, C.S., & Wilsnack, S.C. (1979). Psychosocial characteristics of women with alcoholic fathers. *Currents in Alcoholism, 6,* 209–222.

Beardslee, W.R., Son, L., & Vaillant, G.E. (1986). Exposure to parental alcoholism during childhood and outcome. Adulthood: A prospective longitudinal study. *British Journal of Psychiatry, 149,* 584–591.

Beletsis, S.G., & Brown, S. (1981). A developmental framework for understanding the adult children of alcoholics. *Journal of Addictions and Health, 2*(4), 187–203.

Bell, M.D., Billington, R.J, & Becker, B.R. (1985). Scale for the assessment of reality testing: Reliability, validity and factorial invariance. *Journal of Consulting and Clinical Psychology, 53*(4), 506–511.

Bell, M., Billington, R., & Becker, B. (1986). A scale for the assessment of object relations: Reliability, validity, and factorial invariance. *Journal of Clinical Psychology, 42*(5), 733–741.

Benson, C.S., & Heller, K. (1987). Factors in the current adjustment of young adult daughters of alcoholic and problem drinking fathers. *Journal of Abnormal Psychology, 96*(4), 305–312.

Billings, A.G., Kessler, M., Gomberg, C.A., & Weiner, S. (1979). Marital conflict resolution of alcoholic and nonalcoholic couples during drinking and nondrinking sessions. *Journal of Studies on Alcohol, 40*(3), 183–195.

Bion, W.R. (1961). *Experiences in groups*. New York: Basic Books.

Bion, W.R. (1962). *Learning from experience*. New York: Basic Books.

Black, C. (1981). *It will never happen to me!* Denver: M.A.C. Publications.

Black, C. (1985). *Repeat after me*. Denver: M.A.C. Publications.

Blanck, P.D., & Rosenthal, R. (1984). Mediation of interpersonal expectancy effects: Counselor's tone of voice. *Journal of Educational Psychology, 76*(3), 418–426.

Blanck, P.D., Rosenthal, R., & Vannicelli, M. (1986). Talking to and about patients: The therapist's tone of voice. In P.D. Blanck, R. Buck, & R. Rosenthal (Eds.), *Nonverbal communication in the clinical context*. University Park, PA: Pennsylvania State University Press.

Blane, H.T., & Leonard, K.E. (Eds.). (1987). *Psychological theories of drinking and alcoholism*. New York: Guilford.

Bohman, M., Sigvardsson, S., & Cloninger, R. (1981). Maternal inheritance of alcohol abuse. *Archives of General Psychiatry, 38*(9), 965–969.

Bootzin, R.R. (1985). Affect and cognition in behavior therapy. In S. Reiss & R.R. Bootzin (Eds.), *Theoretical issues in behavior therapy*. Orlando, FL: Academic Press.

Brown, S. (1988). *Treating adult children of alcoholics: A developmental perspective*. New York: Wiley.

Brown, S., & Beletsis, S. (1986). The development of family transference in groups for the adult children of alcoholics. *International Journal of Group Psychotherapy, 36*(1), 97–114.

Brown, S., & Yalom, I.D. (1977). Interactional group therapy with alcoholics. *Journal of Studies on Alcohol, 38*(3), 426–456.

Brownell, K.D., Marlatt, G.A., Lichtenstein, E., & Wilson, G.T. (1986). Understanding and preventing relapse. *American Psychologist, 41*(7), 765–782.

Burk, J.P., & Sher, K.J. (1988). The "forgotten children" revisited: Neglected areas of COA research. *Clinical Psychology Review, 8*, 285–302.

Cahalan, D. (1976). *Problem drinkers: A national survey*. San Francisco: Jossey-Bass.

Cermak, T.L. (1984). Children of alcoholics and the case for a new diagnostic category of codependency. *Alcohol Health and Research World, 8*(4), 38–42.

Cermak, T.L. (1985). *A primer on adult children of alcoholics*. Pompano Beach, FL: Health Communications.

Cermak, T.L., & Brown, S. (1982). Interactional group therapy with the adult children of alcoholics. *International Journal of Group Psychotherapy, 32*(3), 375–389.

Chu, J.A. (1988). *Ten traps for therapists in the treatment of trauma victims.* Paper presented at McLean Hospital, Belmont, MA.

Clark, W.B., & Cahalan, D. (1976). Changes in problem drinking over a four-year span. *Addictive Behaviors, 1,* 251–259.

Cloninger, C.R. (1987). Neurogenetic adaptive mechanisms in alcoholism. *Science, 236,* 410–416.

Cook, D.R. (1985). Craftsman versus professional: Analysis of the controlled drinking controversy. *Journal of Studies on Alcohol, 46*(5), 433–442.

Cooper, D.E. (1987). The role of group psychotherapy in the treatment of substance abusers. *American Journal of Psychotherapy, 41*(1), 55–67.

Cooper, D.E. (1988). *Role requirements of the group psychotherapist: Empathy and neutrality.* Paper presented at the annual meeting of the American Group Psychotherapy Association, New York.

Corder, B.F., McRee, C., & Rohrer, H. (1984). Daughters of alcoholics: A review of the literature. *North Carolina Journal of Mental Health, 10*(20), 37–43.

Davis, D.I., Berenson, D., Steinglass, P., & Davis, S. (1974). The adaptive consequences of drinking. *Psychiatry, 37,* 209–215.

Deutsch, H. (1930). Ein Fall von hysterischer Schicksalsneurose [A case of an hysterical "destiny" neurosis]. *Psychoanalytische Bewegung, 2,* 273–284.

Donovan, J.M (1986). An etiologic model of alcoholism. *American Journal of Psychiatry, 143*(1), 1–11.

Donovan, D.M., & Marlatt, G.A. (1980). Assessment of expectancies and behaviors associated with alcohol consumption. *Journal of Studies on Alcohol, 41*(11), 1153–1185.

Ekman, P., Friesen, V., O'Sullivan, M., & Scherer, K. (1980). Relative importance of face, body, and speech in judgments of personality and affect. *Journal of Personality and Social Psychology, 38*(2), 270–277.

Epstein, L., (1979). The therapeutic use of countertransference data with borderline patients. *Contemporary Psychoanalysis, 15*(2), 248–275.

Fairbairn, W.R.D. (1981). The repression and the return of bad objects. In *Psychoanalytic studies of the personality* (7th ed.). London: Routledge & Kegan Paul. (Original work published in 1943)

Feld, B. (1982). Countertransference in family therapy. *Group, 6*(4), 3–13.

Ferber, A., Mendelsohn, M., & Napier, A. (1972). *The book of family therapy.* New York: Jason Aronson.

Friel, J.C., & Friel, L.D. (1988). *Adult children: The secrets of dysfunctional families.* Deerfield Beach, FL: Health Communications.

Goldstein, A.P. (1960). Therapist and client expectation of personality change in psychotherapy. *Journal of Counseling Psychology, 7*(3), 180–184.

Goodwin, D.W. (1985). Alcoholism and genetics: The sins of the fathers. *Archives of General Psychiatry, 42,* 171–174.

Goodwin, D.W., Schulsinger, F., Hermansen, L., Guze, S.B., & Winokur, G. (1973). Alcohol problems in adoptees raised apart from alcoholic biological parents. *Archives of General Psychiatry, 28,* 238–243.

Gravitz, H.L., & Bowden, J.D. (1984). Therapeutic issues of adult children of alcoholics. *Alcohol Health and Research World, 8*(4), 25–36.

Gravitz, H.L., & Bowden, J.D. (1985). *Guide to recovery: A book for adult children of alcoholics.* Holmes Beach, FL: Learning Publications.

Greenleaf, J. (1981). *Co-alcoholic, para-alcoholic: Who's who and what's the difference?* Denver: M.A.C. Publications.

Griefen, M., Vannicelli, M., & Canning, D. (1985). Treatment contracts in long-term groups with alcoholic outpatients: A group case study. *Group, 9*(3), 43–48.

Grotstein, J. (1981). *Splitting and projective identification.* New York: Jason Aronson.

Guntrip, H. (1969). *Schizoid phenomena, object relations and the self* (7th ed.). New York: International Universities Press.

Hedlund, J.L., & Vieweg, B.W. (1984). The Michigan Alcoholism Screening Test (MAST): A comprehensive review. *Journal of Operational Psychiatry, 15,* 55–65.

Hibbard, S. (1987). The diagnosis and treatment of adult children of alcoholics as a specialized therapeutic population. *Psychotherapy, 24*(4), 779–785.

Imhof, J., Hirsch, R., & Terenzi, R.E. (1983). Countertransferential and attitudinal considerations in the treatment of drug abuse and addiction. *The International Journal of the Addictions, 18*(4), 491–510.

Jacob, T., & Leonard, K. (1986). Psychosocial functioning in children of alcoholic fathers, depressed fathers and control fathers. *Journal of Studies on Alcohol, 47*(5), 373–380.

Johnson Institute. (1987). *How to use intervention in your professional practice.* Minneapolis: Johnson Institute Books.

Kanfer, F.H., & Schefft, B.K. (1988). *Guiding the process of therapeutic change.* Champaign, IL: Research Press.

Kern, J.C. (1985). Management of children of alcoholics. In S. Zimberg, J. Wallace, & S.B. Blume (Eds.), *Practical approaches to alcoholism psychotherapy* (2d ed.). New York: Plenum.

Khantzian, E.J. (1985). Psychotherapeutic interventions with substance abusers — The clinical context. *Journal of Substance Abuse Treatment, 2,* 83–88.

Kissin, B. (1977). Theory and practice in the treatment of alcoholism. In B. Kissin & H. Begleiter (Eds.), *The biology of alcoholism: (Vol. 5) Treatment and rehabilitation of the chronic alcoholic.* New York: Plenum.

Kohut, H. (1971). *The analysis of the self: A systematic approach to the psychoanalytic treatment of narcissistic personality disorders.* New York: International Universities Press.

Kritsberg, W. (1985). *The adult children of alcoholics syndrome: From discovery to recovery.* Pompano Beach, FL: Health Communications.

Krovitz, D. (1987, May-June). Nuts & bolts of recovery: Realistic goals for quality support groups. *Changes,* pp. 12–15.

Langs, R.J. (1975). The therapeutic relationship and deviations in technique. *International Journal of Psychoanalytic Psychotherapy, 4,* 106–141.

Levin, J.D. (1987). *Treatment of alcoholism and other addictions: A self-psychology approach.* Northvale, NJ: Jason Aronson.

Levine, R. (1988). Contributions of countertransference data from the analysis of the Rorschach: An object-relations approach. In H.D. Lerner & P.M. Lerner (Eds.), *Primitive mental states and the rorschach*. Madison, Conn: International Universities Press.

Lewis, D.C., & Williams, C.N. (Eds.). (1986). *Providing care for children of alcoholics*. Clinical and Research Perspectives. Pompano Beach, FL: Health Communications.

Macdonald, D.I., & Blume, S.B. (1986). Children of alcoholics: Editorial review. *American Journal of Diseases of Children, 140, 750–754.*

Malin, A., & Grotstein, J.S. (1966). Projective identification in the therapeutic process. *The International Journal of Psycho-Analysis, 47*(1), 26–31.

Marlatt, G.A. (1985). Relapse prevention: Theoretical rationale and overview of the model. In G. Marlatt & J. Gordon (Eds.), *Relapse prevention: Maintenance, strategies in addictive behavior change*. New York: Guilford.

McConnell, P. (1980). *Adult children of alcoholics: A workbook for healing*. San Francisco: Harper & Row.

McConnell, P. (1986). *A workbook for healing: Adult children of alcoholics*. New York: Harper & Row. (Previously under a slightly different title.)

McDonnell, R., & Callahan, R. (1987). *Hope for healing: Good news for adult children of alcoholics*. New York: Paulist Press.

Mendelson, J.H., & Mello, N.K. (Eds.) (1985). *The diagnosis and treatment of alcoholism* (2d ed.). New York: McGraw-Hill.

Middelton-Moz, J., & Dwinell, L. (1986). *After the tears: Reclaiming the personal losses of childhood*. Pompano Beach, FL: Health Communications.

Miller, W.R. (1983). Motivational interviewing with problem drinkers. *Behavioural Psychotherapy, 11, 147–172.*

Miller, W.R., & Hester, R.K. (1986). Inpatient alcoholism treatment: Who benefits? *American Psychologist, 41*(7), 794–805.

Miller, J.E., & Ripper, M.L. (1988). *Following the yellow brick road: The adult child's personal journey through Oz*. Deerfield Beach, FL: Health Communications.

Moore, R.A. (1965). Some countertransference reactions in the treatment of alcoholism. *Psychiatry Digest, 26, 35–43.*

Moos, R.H., & Billings, A.G. (1982). Children of alcoholics during the recovery process: Alcoholic and matched control families. *Addictive Behaviors, 7, 155–163.*

Moos, R.H., Finney, J.W., & Chan, D.A. (1981). The process of recovery from alcoholism: I. Comparing alcoholic patients and matched community controls. *Journal of Studies on Alcohol, 42*(5), 383–402.

Moos, R.H., & Moos, B.S. (1984). The process of recovery from alcoholism: III. Comparing functioning in families of alcoholics and matched control families. *Journal of Studies on Alcohol, 45*(2), 111–118.

Norwood, R. (1985). *Women who love too much*. New York: Pocket Books, Simon & Schuster.

Orford, J. (1975). Alcoholism and marriage: The argument against specialism. *Journal of Studies on Alcohol, 36*(11), 1537–1563.

Pattison, E.M. (1985). The selection of treatment modalities for the alcoholic patient. In J.H. Mendelson & N.K. Mello (Eds.), *The diagnosis and treatment of alcoholism* (2d ed.). New York: McGraw-Hill.

Peitler, E.J. (1980). A comparison of the effectiveness of group counseling and Alateen on the psychological adjustment of two groups of adolescent sons of alcoholic fathers. (Doctoral dissertation, St. John's University, 1980). *Dissertation Abstracts International, 41*(4), 1520B.

Polich, J.M., Armor, D.J., & Braiker, H.B. (1980). Patterns of alcoholism over four years. *Journal of Studies on Alcohol, 41*(5), 397–416.

Polich, J.M., Armor, D.J., & Braiker, H.B. (1981). *The course of alcoholism four years after treatment.* New York: Wiley.

Racker, H. (1968). *Transference and countertransference.* Madison, CT: International Universities Press.

Russell, M., Henderson, C., & Blume, S.B. (1985). *Children of alcoholics: A review of the literature.* New York: Children of Alcoholics Foundation.

Rutan, J.S., & Stone, W.N. (1984). *Psychodynamic group psychotherapy.* New York: MacMillan.

Rutter, M. (1979). Maternal deprivation, 1972-1978: New findings, new concepts, new approaches. *Child Development, 50,* 283–305.

Saxe, L., Dougherty, D., Esty, J., & Fine, M. (1983). *The effectiveness and costs of alcoholism treatment* (Congressional Office of Technology Assessment Case Study, Publication No. 052-003-00902-1). Washington, DC: U.S. Government Printing Office.

Schuckit, M.A., Li, T.K., Cloninger, C.R., & Deitrich, R.A. (1985). Genetics of alcoholism. *Alcoholism: Clinical and Experimental Research, 9*(6), 475–492.

Searles, H.F. (1979). *Countertransference and related subjects.* New York: International Universities Press.

Seixas, J.S. (1982). Children from alcoholic homes. In N.J. Estes & M.E. Heinemann (Eds.), *Alcoholism: Development, consequences, and interventions* (2d ed.). St. Louis: C.V. Mosby.

Seixas, J.S., & Levitan, M.L. (1984). A supportive counseling group for adult children of alcoholics. *Alcoholism Treatment Quarterly, 1*(4), 123–132.

Seixas, J.S., & Youcha, G. (1985). *Children of alcoholism: A survivor's manual.* New York: Harper & Row.

Selzer, M.L. (1971). The Michigan Alcoholism Screening Test: The quest for a new diagnostic instrument. *American Journal of Psychiatry, 127*(12), 1653–1658.

Selzer, M.L., Vinokur, A., & van Rooijen, L. (1975). A self-administered Short Michigan Alcoholism Screening Test (SMAST). *Journal of Studies on Alcohol, 36*(1), 117–126.

Shay, J.J. (1988). *Rules of thumb for the all-thumbs therapist: A common sense approach.* Paper presented at the Institute for Couples and Families, McLean Hospital, Belmont, MA.

Smith, A.W. (1988). *Grandchildren of alcoholics: Another generation of codependency.* Deerfield Beach, FL: Health Communications.

Snyder, W.V. (1946). "Warmth" in nondirective counseling. *Journal of Abnormal and Social Psychology, 41*(4), 491–495.

Sobell, M.B., & Sobell, L.C. (1973a). Individualized behavior therapy for alcoholics. *Behavior Therapy, 4*(1), 49–72.

Sobell, M.B., & Sobell, L.C. (1973b). Alcoholics treated by individualized behavior therapy: One year treatment outcome. *Behaviour Research and Therapy, 11*, 599–618.

Sobell, M.B., & Sobell, L.C. (1976). Second year treatment outcome of alcoholics treated by individualized behavior therapy: Results. *Behaviour Research and Therapy, 14*(3), 195–215.

Sobell, L.C., Sobell, M.B., & Nirenberg, T.D. (1988). Behavioral assessment and treatment planning with alcohol and drug abusers: A review with an emphasis on clinical application. *Clinical Psychology Review, 8*, 19–54.

Stanton, M.D., & Todd, T.C. (1982). *The family therapy of drug abuse and addiction.* New York: Guilford.

Steinglass, P. (1979). The alcoholic family in the interaction laboratory. *Journal of Nervous and Mental Disease, 167*(7), 428–436.

Steinglass, P., Bennett, L.A., Wolin, S.J., & Reiss, D. (1987). *The alcoholic family.* New York: Basic Books.

Steinglass, P., Davis, D.I., & Berenson, D. (1977). Observations of conjointly hospitalized "alcoholic couples" during sobriety and intoxication: Implications for theory and therapy. *Family Process, 16*, 1–16.

Vaillant, G.E., Clark, W., Cyrus, C., Milofsky, E.S., Kopp, J., Wulsin, V.W., & Mogielnicki, N.P. (1983). Prospective study of alcoholism treatment: Eight-year follow-up. *American Journal of Medicine, 75*, 455–463.

Vannicelli, M. (1987). Treatment of alcoholic couples in outpatient group therapy. *Group, 11*(4), 247–257.

Vannicelli, M. (1988). Group therapy aftercare for alcoholic patients. *International Journal of Group Psychotherapy, 38*(3), 337–353.

Vannicelli, M. (in press). Group psychotherapy with adult children of alcoholics. In M. Seligman & L.A. Marshall (Eds.), *Group psychotherapy: A practitioner's guide to interventions with special populations.* New York: Grune & Stratton.

Vannicelli, M. (1982). Group psychotherapy with alcoholics: Special techniques. *Journal of Studies on Alcohol, 43*(1), 17–37.

Vannicelli, M., Canning, D., & Griefen, M. (1984). Group therapy with alcoholics: A group case study. *International Journal of Group Psychotherapy, 34*(1), 127–147.

Vannicelli, M., Dillavou, D., & Caplan, C. (1988). *Dynamically oriented group therapy with alcoholics: Making it work despite the prevailing bias.* Paper presented at American Group Psychotherapy Association Meeting, New York.

Wegscheider, S. (1984). Children of alcoholics caught in a family trap. *Focus on Alcohol and Drug Issues, 2*, 8.

Wegscheider-Cruse, S. (1985). *Choice-making for co-dependents, adult children and spirituality seekers.* Pompano Beach, FL: Health Communications.

Weisman, M.N., & Robe, L.B. (1983). *Relapse/slips: Abstinent alcoholics who return to drinking.* Minneapolis: Johnson Institute.

Weiss, R.D., & Mirin, S.M. (1987). Substance abuse as an attempt at self-medication. *Psychiatric Medicine, 3,* 357–367.

Werner, E.E. (1986). Resilient offspring of alcoholics: A longitudinal study from birth to age 18. *Journal of Studies on Alcohol, 47*(1), 34–40.

Whitaker, C.A., Felder, R.E., & Warkentin, J. (1965). Countertransference in the family treatment of schizophrenia. In I. Boszormenyi-Nagy & J.L. Framo (Eds.), *Intensive family therapy.* New York: Brunner/Mazel.

Whitfield, C.L. (1987). *Healing the child within: Discovery and recovery for adult children of dysfunctional families.* Deerfield Beach, FL: Health Communications.

Wilson, C., & Orford, J. (1978). Children of alcoholics: Report of a preliminary study and comments on the literature. *Journal of Studies on Alcohol, 39*(1), 121–142.

Winnicott, D.W. (1949). Hate in the countertransference. *The International Journal of Psycho-Analysis, 30*(2), 69–74.

Winnicott, D.W. (1975). Withdrawal and Regression. In *Through paediatrics to psycho-analysis.* New York: Basic Books. (Original work published in 1954)

Winnicott, D.W. (1975). Clinical varieties of transference. In Winnicott, *Through paediatrics to psycho-analysis.* New York: Basic Books. (Original work published in 1955)

Winnicott, D.W. (1965). *The maturational processes and the facilitating environment.* New York: International Universities Press.

Woititz, J.G. (1983). *Adult children of alcoholics.* Pompano Beach, FL: Health Communications.

Woititz, J.G. (1985). *Struggle for intimacy.* Pompano Beach, FL: Health Communications.

Wolin, S.J., Bennett, L.A., & Noonan, D.L. (1979). Family rituals and the recurrence of alcoholism over generations. *American Journal of Psychiatry, 136*(4B), 589–593.

Wolin, S., Steinglass, P., Sendroff, P., Davis, D.I., & Berenson, D. (1975). Marital interaction during experimental intoxication and the relationship to family history. In M. Gross (Ed.), *Experimental studies of alcohol intoxication and withdrawal.* New York: Plenum.

Wood, B.L. (1984). *The COA therapist: When the family hero turns pro.* Paper presented at the meeting of the American Psychological Association, Toronto, Ontario, Canada.

Wood, B.L. (1987). *Children of alcoholism: The struggle for self and intimacy in adult life.* New York: New York University Press.

Wurmser, L. (1981). *The mask of shame.* Baltimore: Johns Hopkins University Press.

Wynne, L.C. (1965). Some indications and contraindications for exploratory family therapy. In I. Boszormenyi-Nagy & J.L. Framo (Eds.), *Intensive family therapy.* New York: Brunner/Mazel.

Yalom, I.D. (1975). *The theory and practice of group psychotherapy* (2d ed.). New York: Basic Books.

Zimberg, S. (1982). Psychotherapy in the treatment of alcoholism. In E.M. Pattison & E. Kaufman (Eds.), *Encyclopedic handbook of alcoholism*. New York: Gardner.

Zucker, R.A., & Gomberg, E.S.L. (1986). Etiology of alcoholism reconsidered: The case for a biopsychosocial process. *American Psychologist, 41*(7), 783–793.

Zucker, R.A. (1987). The four alcoholisms: A developmental account of the etiologic process. In C. Rivers (Ed.), *Alcohol and addictive behavior: Nebraska Symposium on Motivation, 1986*. Lincoln: University of Nebraska Press.

Index

217